Writing Business Plans That Get Results

A Step-by-Step Guide

MICHAEL O'DONNELL

CB
CONTEMPORARY BOOKS

Library of Congress Cataloging-in-Publication Data

O'Donnell, Michael, 1957–
    Writing business plans that get results: a step-by-step guide
Michael O'Donnell.
       p.   cm.
    Includes bibliographical references.
    ISBN 0-8092-4007-6
    1. New business enterprises—Finance.   2. New business
enterprises—Planning.   I. Title.
HG4027.6.036   1991
658.4'012—dc20   91-9820
                      CIP

Published by Contemporary Books
A division of NTC/Contemporary Publishing Group, Inc.
4255 West Touhy Avenue, Lincolnwood (Chicago), Illinois 60712-1975 U.S.A.
Copyright © 1991, 1988 by Center for Innovation and Business Development
Printed in the United States of America
ISBN 978-0-07-183162-8
09 10 IBT/IBT 26 25 24 23 22 21 20 19

Dedicated to you—the entrepreneur.

You are among a rare and inspiring breed
of individuals who are redefining the way
America lives and works.

Contents

Acknowledgments

M any important people took time from their busy schedules to review the first draft of this guide. They offered a lot of insights into the trials and tribulations of starting a new business. Looking over the list, you will find they make up an impressive group of professionals, representing all areas of business disciplines. We gratefully acknowledge their assistance.

Doug Betlach—Small Business Management Coordinator, North Valley Vocational Center

Leonard Christianson—Technical Director, Center for Innovation

Leon F. Dubourt—Chairman of the Board, Walhalla State Bank

Michael J. Gallagher—Business Development Specialist, U.S. Small Business Administration

Jon Geyerman—President, Norman Jessen and Associates, Inc.

Bruce Gjovig—Director, Center for Innovation and Business Development

Marv Kaiser—Attorney-at-Law

Patrick Marx—Minnesota World Trade Center

Robert W. Nelson—President, Grand Forks Development Foundation

Garry A. Pearson—Pearson and Christensen, Attorneys-at-Law

Tom Rolfstad—Economic Development Planner, North Dakota Economic Development Commission

Bill Schott—Development Coordinator, Basin Electric Corporation

Lyle C. Sorum—Vice President, Director of Marketing, Bremer Financial Service, Inc.

Dave Stenseth—President, Sioux Falls Development Corporation

Reed A. Stigen—CPA, Charles Bailly and Company

Chuck Stroup—Vice President, Union State Bank

Jerry Udell, Ph.D—Professor of Marketing, Minutemen Graduate Program, UND

Richard Wold—President, First National Bank

Special thanks to Sandy Kovar for her patience and dedication in typing the many drafts.

Preface

"Never tell people how *to do things.*
Tell them what *to do and they will*
surprise you with their ingenuity."
General George S. Patton

This quote is fitting for today's entrepreneurial spirit and reflects the spirit of this publication. America is experiencing a boom in new business start-ups. Entrepreneurs are the heroes. They develop new products, they encourage innovation, they create new jobs. Unfortunately, many of them fail because they don't know what they are getting into to begin with. This knowledge gap has given rise to "entrepreneurial consultants" and "new business experts." There are probably as many "professional advisers" out there as there are new business start-ups. Because each new business start-up is different, a lot of this advice is confusing and even conflicting.

This business planning guide is a series of exercises. It tells you *what* to do (or be thinking about), not *how* to do it. Starting a business requires perseverance. You must take initiative and utilize whatever resources are available to you. We don't have all the answers, and there is no way we can tell you where to go to find them without making this publication so voluminous that it would be unreadable. The guide may be imposing for some as is, but it is so by necessity. Writing a business plan can be a time-consuming and tedious task. It can also be very enlightening and rewarding. No matter what your objective may be with a start-up venture, you stand a much better chance of profiting from it with a well-thought-out business plan.

This guide was written to help you identify basic issues, address the details, and write a comprehensive business plan. First and foremost, it is a guide that recognizes that effective business plans must be tailored to unique circumstances. Many how-to publications and seminars are being promoted about business planning that do not truly embrace this simple fact in their material. They may be good for motivating people, but usually they neglect the details involved in starting or expanding a venture, along with the features that make it unique. Each venture has its own problems and opportunities, and each must address distinct issues that are separate from other kinds of start-ups.

Introduction

**How High
Can You Jump?**

You need to feel comfortable with why you must go through the exercise of writing a business plan. If you don't understand the reasons for it and the benefits it will bring, in all likelihood you will do a less-than-adequate job. You will defeat your purpose before you ever get started. To be sure, writing a business plan is one of those hoops you must jump through. The players (investors, customers, suppliers, etc.) are simply not going to let you play until you are good enough to be on the team. Besides, if you can't put your plan on paper, then you haven't really thought it out. You may think this is an exercise in futility, especially since times and events change and your company will certainly change with them. But that is exactly why you need to have a business plan.

Your plan must reflect your ultimate goal. Be honest up front. What will be the extent of your involvement? Do you want to own and/or manage this start-up? If so, be prepared to show why you are capable and how you will compensate in the areas in which you have no expertise. Perhaps your real aim is to sell your idea or license your product to an existing company in exchange for royalties. Your plan must be written according to what *you* want. You must then tailor it to a specific use.

**The Uses of a
Business Plan**

Your plan can accomplish many things for you and your proposed venture, but it is not prudent to try to make it be all things to all people. One plan will simply not suffice for all possible uses. Indeed, most seasoned entrepreneurs will write (or revise) a business plan at each stage of the company's development. The most successful of these will then write several plans, each adapted to specific players.

Sounds like a pain, doesn't it? Actually, it is not that difficult or time-consuming. Once you have done your homework and decided to go ahead, it doesn't take much more effort to expand and/or adapt a business plan. The basic format of a plan is essentially the same for all uses. The trick is to beef up the sections that are of most interest to your target audience: investors, the management team, suppliers, customers, etc.

A Development Tool

A plan of this nature is written for you, your partner(s) if you have any, and any other principals concerned with the start-up. You will want to concentrate on the section dealing with overall schedule and milestones (Module 12). This plan functions as a detailed "to do" list. It helps you set realistic deadlines and delegate assignments. It keeps you on track in the early stages.

At this point the other sections of your plan are sketchy, just some initial thoughts on how you think the whole venture will come together (or would like it to). It serves as a blueprint for filling in the details in the other sections and substantiating how and why your idea will be successful. If your objective is to develop your idea just far enough to prove it feasible, sell it, and go on to something else, then tailor your plan to that objective.

A Management and Planning Guide

If you're in for the long haul, this is the plan you want to develop. This use is at the heart of all good plans. Since it is the most comprehensive, most of the other uses of a business plan are adapted from this one.

This type of plan becomes an operating bible for the *management* of your company. Since you can't predict the future, the best you can do is monitor and measure actual performance against expected performance. When events deviate from your plan, you can quickly take corrective action.

This use forces you to identify opportunities and threats, strengths and weaknesses. It will prompt you and your associates to agree on goals, strategies, and objectives in a systematic and realistic manner. You will want to concentrate on the sections dealing with operations, management and ownership, and administration, organization, and personnel (Modules 9, 10, and 11).

A Mission Statement

No matter what stage of development your idea may be in, you are going to have to let certain key people know what you are all about. This type of plan is used to team up with suppliers, to inform consultants and other professionals that may be needed (lawyers, accountants, etc.), and to precommit customers. You will not always be granted a forum to explain in person what they need to know to act on your idea. You should always be prepared to give them a plan to review—one that is tailored to their interest or expertise.

An overview of each section may be appropriate, but you may not want to share detailed or confidential information with certain parties. For suppliers it may be appropriate to beef up the sections on the product and the technological or manufacturing operations or it may be that if suppliers knew these things, they could pose a competitive threat. Use your judgment, giving each player a plan that goes into detail in sections that are applicable to that player while giving only a brief sketch of the other sections.

A Sales Document

The vast majority of business plans are written exclusively for this use. Most end up as nothing more than shallow sales material. Sophisticated investors recognize these right away and pitch them in the circular file. No one can deny that a good business plan is one that raises money. But all sections must be well researched and documented, and financial projections and assumptions must be substantiated.

If you're going to romance money, you have to appeal. The problem is, what excites one person doesn't necessarily excite another. Again, you will have to tailor this kind of plan to the type of financing you are seeking (or think you stand the best chance of getting). It is not unusual for some entrepreneurs to cover all the bases by writing several plans, each designed to address the interests and concerns of the different financial groups.

Bankers, for instance, are usually more conservative than venture capitalists and private investors. Bankers will be interested primarily in the company's fixed assets (building, equipment, etc.) and the collateral you can offer. They often don't care how innovative your idea is, what industry you are in, or how many trillions of dollars you are going to make. They just want to know if their loan can be paid back at the going interest rate.

Venture capitalists (and other sophisticated independent investment groups, by any other name) are more willing to roll the dice. They may want a chunk of your company and its profits for their risk. They like innovative products and services that address a growth or "glamour" industry. They want to earn at least a 45 percent compounded annual return on investment (ROI, one of those catchy terms people like to see in a business plan). *In other words, they want to get back six times their money in three to five years.* The sections to beef up for this use are, in order of importance, the Executive Summary, the Financial Data and Projections (particularly a current balance sheet and terms of the deal), Management and Ownership, and the Product and Related Services.

Private investors are the most common financiers of start-ups. They are usually family, friends, and other well-wishers who want you out of their hair but have a sincere desire to see you succeed. These people can't be taken for granted. Many of today's most successful companies were started in garages just this way. Private investors deserve to see a plan, especially if you want them to take you seriously. After all, business is business.

Limited partnerships and other types of deals can also be structured through more sophisticated private investors. If you are targeting local investors to fund your start-up, they will look for who else is in the deal. They like to see a big name they know (or have heard of) and respect. You will want to beef up the Management and Ownership section, particularly the board of directors.

Very simply, a plan tells the reader where you have been, where you are now, and where you hope to go. Don't worry about raising money at this point. Money will be attracted to a good business idea that feasibly can be implemented. Plenty of avenues are open. Your first objective is to write a good plan that can be tailored to a specific use. Just don't lose sight of the fact that you are writing the plan as much for yourself as for anyone else.

Who Should Write the Plan?

You should write the business plan.

So you may not be a literary genius. That's not the point. It is the process, not the writing, that counts. If someone else writes the plan, then it is *his* plan, not *yours*. The people interested in this start-up want to see that you know and understand the functional areas of a company. They want to be sure you have the big picture and will pay attention to the details as well. If you cannot write it for lack of time or circumstance, you should maintain as much control over and direction of the writing as possible.

"Remember, people buy people. . . . Most products and services cannot be patented. . . . Contrary to popular belief, you can build a better mousetrap, but the world will *not* beat a path to your door. . . . A plan is only as good as the people who implement it. . . . Investors put more stock in the management than in the product. That is why there is generally more money chasing well-developed ideas than there are ideas chasing money. . . ." These statements are all clichés often heard in the venture capital world. They are reinforced here because they are all true.

Investors know that if your business plan is not done right, you probably will never do anything of substance beyond it. This guide gives you what you need to demonstrate the credibility and competence of a workable plan. The confidence and commitment to get through it can come only from you. In this sense the guide serves as architect and engineer. It will help you build a well-designed plan that is structurally sound. You're the builder. What you put into it—the thought, research, facts and figures, and other information—are the bricks and mortar.

Authenticity and Style

You may have noticed that this guide takes an unusually informal and personal approach. It is unique because it doesn't look or sound like a textbook. Its purpose is to communicate with you, not impress you with complicated theories and formulas.

Your business plan is uniquely yours. Use your own style. It should be a personal expression (an art form) as much as a professional document (scientifically and structurally sound). Feel free to express yourself in the first person (we, I, ours). In your first draft, do not be overly concerned with spelling, punctuation, and grammar. Let the writing flow naturally from your heart and mind, utilizing your research notes and experience. Someone who writes well can help you put the finishing touches on it later. For an excellent guide to writing, check out *Elements of Style*, Strunk and White. This paperback should be available through your local library.

You will want your work to transmit enthusiasm, but try to avoid using flowery language and superlatives. Phrases like "fantastic sales" and "tremendous profits" send up red flags and will lessen the impact of truly significant messages. There are certain words and phrases that investors and other professionals do look for (like ROI), and a glossary is included to help you understand the lingo. Incorporate them into your text in your own way. Above all, use clear layman's language. Remember, some of the people who will be reading your plan will know nothing about your product, the technological or manufacturing process involved, or even the industry it addresses.

Writing One That Works

Writing a business plan is tough work. A typical time frame for writing a plan would exceed 300 hours over one to six months, depending on how much time can be devoted to the research and writing. The plan must be comprehensive but concise. Only in exceptional cases should it exceed 50 pages (typewritten/single-spaced); 25 pages would be a good target. A too-sketchy plan will be viewed as evidence the entrepreneur has not done his or her homework—sure grounds for rejection. If it is too long and brought in on a wheelbarrow, it won't be read, which is the same as rejection. You have to write a plan that people will read and that will give them confidence in you and your idea.

The Executive Summary

The most important section of your business plan is the Executive Summary. After months of work, if you haven't sold the business opportunity in the first five minutes of reading, you have lost your reader. If not excited on the first two pages, the reader certainly won't hunt through the chapters for what makes your venture truly unique and worthy of support. The Executive Summary should highlight the most significant points of your business plan and entice the reader to read on. In six paragraphs, the following need to be described:

1. Your product and why it is unique and profitable

2. What business you are in and the milestones reached with financial results

3. What the market is for your product, what size it will be, and your share of the market

4. The management team and their expertise

5. What the financial terms and profit potential are

6. What your unique strengths and advantages are that will contribute to the success of this venture

It is best to write the Executive Summary after you have written the rest of the business plan, because that exercise will also help you sort out the important information.

Financial Information

The next most important portion of the business plan is the Financial Data and Projections—after all, you are in business for profits. The financial section should clearly indicate the amount of funds needed and what those funds would be used for. This section is highly scrutinized by the people with money. If the company is already in operation, you will need to provide a profit and loss statement and a balance sheet. An existing or start-up company needs to provide projections for these statements for a three- to five-year period. These statements should indicate the upside, downside, and expected financial results.

It is also to your advantage to provide a break-even analysis. The five-year requirement may seem impossible to meet with any accuracy and often is. One solution is to generate three scenarios for the five-year period. Use conservative projections based on weak market performance, aggressive projections based on robust demand, and the most likely results of your efforts. It is also recommended that you explain key assumptions and show how the numbers were derived. Prepare to justify your figures.

The Management Team

After the reader has summed up the unique business opportunity and the financial projections, the final determination is whether the entrepreneur can really do the job. The credibility of the business plan will be under siege, and if it survives the analysis, the focus will be on the entrepreneur and whether he or she can meet company objectives and make money. The Management and Ownership section of the business plan must outline experience, expertise, and past accomplishments, and the tone of the business plan must be honest and evoke trust. The entrepreneur has to identify the weaknesses and negatives and address them. The reader wants to reduce his risk, and he wants to know if you are doing that.

If the reader is still with you, he will finish reading the business plan with a critical eye. If you have managed, however, to romance your reader, he may be looking for the reasons why he should support your business opportunity. If interested, he is selling himself and justifying his decision. Write the rest of the chapters well and give readers the reasons they should be involved.

What to Avoid

Most bankers, investors, venture capitalists, and consultants have too much to do in too little time, so entrepreneurs need to avoid the turnoffs often associated with business plans. We have already talked about the plan's being too long or too short. The business plan needs to be "crisp," indicating clearly and concisely what this venture is all about. Readers expect a professional business plan, neatly typed with no spelling errors, but a too-polished business plan with a fancy cover raises eyebrows and red flags. The emphasis should be on substance, not on form and style. Other turnoffs include a poor marketing plan, failure to identify details about competitors, failure to identify key employees, weaknesses in the management team, massive advertising budgets, high salaries, and unrealistic sales forecasts.

Remember, you want to push the hot button of your reader, not raise flags and eyebrows. Do your homework, evaluate the plan critically, and check it again. Whether the reader is you, your partners, your uncle Harry, the banker, or a venture capitalist, your business plan is written for a good purpose.

In Summary

A business plan is a necessary exercise, often required by investors, suppliers, and customers. Most importantly, it is a vital planning tool for the entrepreneur.

- A business plan must reflect the entrepreneur's ultimate goal for the venture.

- A business plan may be tailored for several uses:

  - as a development tool for the founders

  - as a planning and evaluation guide for the managers and other key people

  - as a mission statement to inform key audiences

  - as a sales document for raising capital

- Expect to spend a minimum of 300 hours developing the business plan. Planning is a vital component to position a new venture properly and strategically. It is your road map to business success.

- By the way, some people will tell you that researching and writing a business plan that results in the successful start-up of a company is equivalent to an MBA degree any day. While this statement is certainly debatable, no one can argue that the experience isn't an educational one. An exciting one at that. Good luck and many happy revenues!

The Modular Approach

A Word on Format

This guide is written in modular format, with each module representing a chapter or section of a good business plan. Each module is designed to stand alone. It assumes that people collect, organize, and absorb information in blocks rather than in large doses. While keeping the big picture in perspective, this guide attempts to make writing the business plan a series of minilessons. Work on one module at a time. There is no reason to frustrate yourself with too much material or information at once.

Some modules may not apply to you. If yours is a service business, the module on product manufacturing will be of little interest. Pick and choose what you need. Most of the modules are part of a well-designed business plan that must be addressed by all start-up companies in any industry. Depending on the scope of the venture, it may be appropriate to combine and condense several modules into one section.

Each module breaks down the essential components of a business plan. They are presented in logical sequence, in workbook fashion.

Suggested Length of the Section

This is purely a judgment call. Use as much space as you need, but be concise and to the point. Business plans fewer than 10 pages long have been known to raise millions, but rarely. Again, the length will be determined largely by the intended use of the plan. Avoid the wheelbarrow approach. These plans are so long that you need two people to lift them. Too much information is as damaging as too little information. It only confuses and overwhelms the reader. All totaled, your plan should not exceed 50 pages (not including appendixes) typewritten and single-spaced.

Objective of the Module

This is why the entire module was written.

Questions That Must be Answered

This part of each module is the most important aspect of this guide. The questions are thought provokers. They are not all-inclusive. They do not cover *every* issue you might be concerned with, but they cover at least the basics and will lead you to uncover and address other issues. The questions not only help you discover issues you should include in your business plan; they also prepare you for the verbal firing line when you go before prospective investors. These are the questions that *will* be asked of you—you can count on it! No one expects you to have all the answers. They *do* expect you to know most of the questions and want to know how you are thinking about attacking these issues. (Some of the same issues are covered in two or more modules. Therefore, you will find some redundancy. To be thorough and allow each module to stand alone, this couldn't be avoided.)

Subheadings to Include

These simply highlight the most important aspects of each module of your business plan. Subheadings help make your plan more readable. The subheadings we recommend are standard issues of each topic. They are only suggestions. Include whatever subheadings you think appropriate for your situation.

Description of What to Accomplish Under Each Subheading

This is *how* each issue will be addressed. It is a guide to refer to as you outline and write each module. Again, it is not all-inclusive. Your gut feelings and unique style will be your best guide as you develop and write each module.

A List of Common Mistakes to Avoid

This will help you ensure the integrity of each module of your plan. Most plans fail because of the same pitfalls and weaknesses. These lists try to identify most of them for you. You may want to glance over them *before* you write each module. After you write each module, study this list closely and recheck your work. It is also wise to have an objective friend or adviser look over the list and then read what you have written. Such people will be more apt to pick up on common mistakes.

The sequence of topics in each module was chosen carefully. Research indicates this sequence is preferred by investors, bankers, and other professionals, although it is not carved in stone. The sequence of the contents of your plan, however, is entirely up to you. A reader who has a particular interest in a certain module can find it in the table of contents and go right to it.

There is one trap to avoid as you begin. **The sequence in which your plan's contents will appear is not necessarily the order in which you will research and write each module.** For example, the Executive Summary appears first but is usually the last module to be written. The first thing you need is market information. Second, can your idea be put into a *profitable* plan of action? Therefore, the market research and financial projections are usually most important. All other modules are developed from these.

Suggestions on How to Proceed

1. Flip through this entire guide to acquaint yourself with the modules. Decide if you should combine one or more modules into one section (see Module 2—The Table of Contents).

2. Decide where you would like to (or should) begin. Complete one module at a time. It is suggested that you start with Module 3 or 6.

3. Make sure you understand the objective of each module. Keep the objective foremost in your mind as you write that module of your plan.

4. Read through each module carefully, noting areas where you will have to do some additional research before you are able to answer the questions. If a question does not apply to your situation, you should cross it out. This will help you keep a positive attitude by making your task appear less tedious.

5. Pick up your pencil and go to work! You should not expect to complete each module on your first attempt, but do as much as you can the first time through.

6. Continue to work on the questions not yet answered until you have completed the module. Do not feel constrained by the space allowed for each question. If you need additional space, write either in the margins or on a separate sheet of paper.

7. Decide on the subheadings you want to include in each module. Using the description of what to accomplish as a guide, outline each subheading according to your research and experience as reflected by your answers to the questions.

8. Write each module of the business plan in your own style according to the outlines provided.

9. Critique your work for each module using the list of common mistakes to avoid.

10. Have your plan proofread by a person well versed in English grammar. Have it reviewed by your accountant and other professional advisers. Finally, have it bound in an attractive binder (see "Packaging Your Business Plan" in the "Finishing Touches" chapter).

Module 1—The Executive Summary

Suggested Length	1–3 pages
Objective	To get the reader to keep on reading; to highlight the most significant points of each module.
Pertinent Questions	1. What type of venture is this? (Check and describe.)

    ☐ merchandising

    ☐ manufacturing/processing

    ☐ distribution

    ☐ service

    ☐ other _____

_____

_____

_____

2. What products/services will it offer?

_____

_____

_____

Why are they unique?

_____

_____

_____

Do they solve a significant problem?

_____

_____

_____

Do they address a major opportunity?

_____

_____

_____

3. What is the business status? (Check and describe.)
   ☐ start-up
   ☐ takeover
   ☐ expansion
   ☐ other _____

   _____

   _____

   _____

   _____

4. What stage is this venture in? (Check and describe.)
   ☐ research and development
   ☐ prototype
   ☐ operational _____

   _____

   _____

   _____

5. How long has the business been operating (or been in development)?

   _____ months   _____ years

6. What will be the form of organization? (Check and describe.)
   ☐ proprietorship
   ☐ partnership (type?)
   ☐ corporation (type?)

   _____

   _____

   _____

   _____

7. Where will the business be located?

   _____

   _____

   _____

   What is advantageous about this location?

   _____

   _____

   _____

8. Who and what is the target market?

_____

_____

_____

_____

_____

9. What percent of the available market will you obtain?

_____

_____

_____

What is your plan and strategy for entering the market?

_____

_____

_____

_____

_____

10. Who is the competition?

_____

_____

_____

_____

_____

What are their strengths and weaknesses?

_____

_____

_____

_____

_____

What is their market share?

_____

_____

_____

11. Who is going to manage the business?

_____

_____

_____

_____

What qualifications are needed to manage this business?

_____

_____

_____

_____

What is the experience, education, and background of the principals?

_____

_____

_____

_____

12. What are the time frames for accomplishing the milestones and goals?

_____

_____

_____

_____

13. How much money is needed to make this venture successful?

_____

_____

_____

How much money is needed for product improvement?

_____

_____

_____

How much money is needed for marketing?

_____

_____

_____

How much money is needed for operations?

_____

_____

_____

14. What kind of financing are you looking for? (Check and describe.)
    ☐ debt
    ☐ equity

    _____

    _____

    _____

15. What are you offering in return? (Check and describe.)
    ☐ ownership (how much?)
    ☐ share of profits (projected earnings over 3–5 years)
    ☐ other _____

    _____

    _____

    _____

16. What is the payback period?

    _____

    _____

    _____

17. How much money has been invested to date?

    _____

    _____

    _____

18. What is your interest (financial and otherwise) and long-term objective?

    _____

    _____

    _____

    _____

19. What are the strengths of the business (what will make it successful)? (Check and describe.)

    ☐ management

    ☐ skilled/experienced personnel

    ☐ unique product/service

    ☐ constant source of supply

    ☐ low production/overhead

    ☐ high margin

    ☐ good service

    ☐ emphasis on quality

    _____

    _____

    _____

    _____

    _____

20. What are the limitations on the business? (Check and describe.)

    ☐ capital

    ☐ management resources

    ☐ personnel

    ☐ other _____

    _____

    _____

    _____

    _____

21. What are the venture's long-range growth and expansion objectives?

    _____

    _____

    _____

    _____

    _____

Subheadings to Include

The Executive Summary is one complete module. A summary Fact Sheet at the back of the section is recommended. The subheads should match the major headings or subjects you've covered in your business plan.

What to Accomplish

The entire summary should be clear and to the point. Use short, choppy phrases. The language should be simple and demonstrate clarity of management objectives. Above all, the summary should *show opportunity*!

The following is a suggested sequence of presentation:

Concept

The opening statement should grab attention. State something about being the first to introduce this product or the customer demands being generated from your initial market research. Describe the nature of the business, i.e., type, location, business form, length, and state of operation. Describe current milestones reached and their financial results, i.e., reaching x amount in sales, evaluation and testing completed, prototype built. State what industry your product addresses.

Product/Service

Describe your product. Discuss specialization and significant or unique features. Discuss where you are or would like to be located. State why this location will be advantageous. If the product is to be sold or distributed through other outlets, discuss how this will be done and the outlets' locations. Describe any precommitted sales or contractual relationships you have with manufacturers and/or distributors for your product.

Market

Describe the market for your product, your current or projected share, and overall potential. Discuss the competition and what advantages you have over them. Discuss your plans for introducing your product and your strategy for gaining market acceptance and loyalty. Mention any letters of intent you have with prospective customers.

Manufacturing/Operations

Discuss the processes involved in producing your product and getting it into the marketplace. Highlight areas of specialization and technology that you may have pioneered in the production of the product. If you plan to subcontract or license manufacturing/operations, describe the arrangement and why it is advantageous.

Management

Discuss the people involved in the venture, their management expertise and experience. Highlight their distinctive competence. Discuss support personnel that will be needed as the company grows. Show that the people involved are qualified and committed.

Funding Request and Times of Investment

State how much money has been invested in the venture to date. State the additional funds needed and their use. Discuss what you are offering in return for the money. Include the payback period and potential return on investment. State what the earning projections are for the next three to five years. State any tax benefits that will result from investment.

Milestones and Time Frames

State what must be done and the expected completion date to move the venture along. Describe the phases and time frames with which the business will be concerned. Summarize the unique advantages and strengths that will contribute to the success of the venture.

Common Mistakes to Avoid

- Being too wordy; not to the point
- Being too long; trying to be all-inclusive
- Failing to identify a special or unique opportunity
- Failing to demonstrate clearly what the venture is all about
- Failing to identify what management hopes to accomplish and how it plans to go about it
- Making terms of the deal unclear
- Failing to ensure all the proper legal steps have been taken (see Fact Sheet)

The Fact Sheet stands alone and appears at the back of the Executive Summary module as a separate page. It enables the reader to scan the vital information that makes up the company. Fill in the following Fact Sheet and have it typed on a separate page.

Fact Sheet

Name of Company:

Location (address, city, county, state, zip, phone):

Zoning Classification (obtain from city ordinance):

Type of Business and Industry (examples—manufacturing, agriculture):

Business Form (proprietorship, partnership [type], corporation [type]:

Product or Service Line (examples—electronics, household):

Patent, Trademark, or Service Mark (type, number, date issued):

Length of Time in Business (or in development):

Number of Founders/Partners/Employees:

Current and/or Projected Share of Market (examples—10% of market 1985, 20% 1986):

Invested to Date (estimate equipment, supplies, time):

Net Worth:

Additional Financing Needed (estimate total dollar amount):

Minimum Investment (dollar amount for stock, partnership unit, etc.):

Terms and Payback Period (example—equity position, limited partnership shares, 3-year buyback, 40% ROI):

Total Valuation (after placement):

Legal Counsel:

Financial Counsel:

Management Counsel:

Description of any related party transactions, contracts, or relationships that the company may be involved in

Module 2—The Table of Contents

Suggested Length	1–2 pages
Objective	To allow the reader to quickly access particular sections of interest
Pertinent Questions	1. What are the pertinent sections (topics) that you should include in your plan?
	What are the appropriate subheadings for each?
	2. In what order will you present the contents?
	3. What pictures, graphs, legal documents, etc., should you include as supporting material?
	4. Given the nature of the business and purpose for which you are writing the plan, how long (number of pages) will this plan be?
Subheadings to Include	The following is a list of topics or issues you might include. Depending on the importance of each issue to your start-up, any one can stand alone as a separate section or be combined with another issue. Also listed are possible subheadings that may be organized under each main topic.

The Company
>Background
>Current Status
>Future Plans

The Industry
>Chief Characteristics
>The Participants
>Analyst Summaries
>Trends

Product and Related Services
>Product/Service Description
>Facilities Description
>Proprietary Features
>Future Development Plans
>Product Liability

Technology: Research and Development
Concept Development
Research, Testing, and Evaluation
Milestones and Breakthroughs
Current Status and Continuing R&D

Market Analysis
Target Market and Characteristics
Analyst Summaries
Market Share, Trends, and Growth Potential
Sales, Distribution, and Profits by Product/Service

Competitive Analysis
Competitors' Profile
Product/Service Comparison
Market Niche and Share
Comparison of Strengths and Weaknesses

Marketing Strategy
Penetration Goals
Pricing and Packaging
Sales and Distribution
Service and Warranty Policies
Advertising, Public Relations, and Promotions

Manufacturing Process and Operations
Location
Facilities and Equipment
Manufacturing Process and Operations
Labor Considerations
Environmental and Economic Impact

Management and Ownership
Key People and Experience
Board of Directors
Ownership Distribution and Incentives
Professional Support Services

Administration, Organization, and Personnel
Administrative Procedures and Controls
Staffing and Training
Organizational Chart
Management Control Systems

Milestones, Schedule, and Strategic Planning
Major Milestones (What/Why)
Schedule (When/Who)
Strategic Planning (How/Where)

Critical Risks and Problems
    Summary of Major Problems Overcome
    Inevitable Risks and Problems
    Potential Risks and Problems
    Worst-Case Scenarios

Financial Data and Projections
    Funding Request/Terms of Investment
    Current Financial Statements
    Financial Projections
    Assumptions

Appendixes

The following is a condensed version of the Table of Contents utilizing all the modules.

Executive Summary
  I. Business Summary
    A. The Company and the Industry
    B. Management and Ownership
    C. Administration, Organization, and Personnel

  II. The Product and Services
    A. The Technology: Research and Development
    B. Manufacturing and Operations

  III. The Market
    A. Market Analysis
    B. Competitive Analysis
    C. Marketing Strategy

  IV. Schedule and Risks

  V. Financial Data

  VI. Appendixes

What to Accomplish   All major sections should be listed in bold print in the order in which they appear in the plan. Designate each major section with a Roman numeral along the left-hand margin. All major sections and subheadings should have a corresponding page number listed along the right-hand margin. Example:

**Common Mistakes
to Avoid**

■ Prominent sections of interest are not discernible

■ Page numbers are not clearly marked for each section

■ Sequence of topic presentation follows a confusing or an illogical pattern

■ Certain subheadings are listed under unrelated major sections

Module 3—The Company and the Industry

Suggested Length   1–3 pages

Objective   To describe the start-up and background of your company. To provide a brief sketch of your industry and how your venture addresses it.

Note: The first part of this module is primarily for ventures that have some operating history. If your company has a significant history, you may want to have this section stand alone as its own chapter.

Pertinent Questions   1. When and where was the company started?

_____

_____

_____

Date and state of incorporation or partnership?

_____

_____

_____

2. What is the form of organization?

_____

_____

_____

Will this be changing? When?

_____

_____

_____

3. Where is the business located?

_____

_____

_____

Will you change, or have you changed, locations?

_____

Why? _____

_____

_____

4. How long have you been in business?

_____

_____

_____

5. Did you obtain a patent or trademark for the company's name
   and/or logo?

_____

Do you have one pending? _____

6. Why did you go into business?

_____

_____

_____

7. How was this business venture developed?

_____

_____

_____

How long did it take? _____

What problems were encountered?

_____

_____

_____

How were they overcome?

_____

_____

_____

_____

What were the key milestones?

_____

_____

_____

How and when were they accomplished?

_____

_____

_____

_____

8. Who are the founders and other key people involved?

_____

_____

_____

_____

What do they bring to the business?

_____

_____

_____

_____

_____

9. How did you identify your market?

_____

_____

_____

_____

What success have you had in penetrating it?

_____

_____

_____

_____

10. How have you dealt with the competition?

_____

_____

_____

_____

11. What are your overall strengths and weaknesses?

_____

_____

_____

_____

12. How much money have you invested?

_____

_____

_____

What has been your source of funding?

_____

_____

_____

How has the money been used?

_____

_____

_____

Is the investment secured? How?

_____

_____

13. What are your future goals and strategies for achieving them?

_____

_____

_____

_____

_____

14. How is your company affected by major economic, social, technological, environmental, or regulatory trends?

_____

_____

_____

_____

_____

_____

15. What is your sales and service record?

_____

_____

_____

_____

16. What industry are you in?

_____

_____

17. What is the current state of the industry?

_____

_____

_____

How big is it?

_____

Total sales? profits? margins?

_____

_____

18. Who are the major industry participants (competitors, suppliers, major customers, distributors, etc.)?

_____

_____

_____

_____

What is their performance? market share?

_____

_____

_____

_____

What advantages do you have over them?

_____

_____

_____

_____

How will you capture markets others are competing for?

_____

_____

_____

_____

19. What are the industry's chief characteristics?

_____

_____

_____

_____

Where is it expected to be in 5 years? 10 years?

_____

_____

_____

_____

Will your share increase or decrease with these changes?

_____

_____

_____

Who else may get into the industry?

_____

_____

_____

Subheadings to
Include

The Company
      Background
      Current Status
      Future Plans

The Industry
      Chief Characteristics
      The Participants
      Analyst Summaries
      Trends

What to Accomplish

Make the reader a part of your dreams. Describe how your work and decisions got the company where it is. Show how past performance will pave the way to future success. Demonstrate how you will become an important addition to the industry and that you understand the industry and where it is headed.

The following is a suggested sequence of presentation:

The Company

Background

Describe the start-up and history of your company from the time of inception. State where and when it was organized. State what form of business it is and where it is located. Discuss significant milestones, such as obtaining a patent, building a prototype, or signing a major contract. Discuss the people involved and the roles they have played. Mention any trademarks on the company's name or logo.

Current Status

Discuss where you are now. Talk about the reputation you have built, your strengths, and what limitations are being experienced. Describe how your product is performing in the marketplace. State the amount of money that has been invested to date, by whom, and how it has been used. Give an overview of your sales and services record, if any. Discuss the kind and amount of funding the business needs to begin operations or improve operations.

Future Plans

Discuss your goals for the next three to five years. Describe how you plan to achieve them and what resources will be needed. Allude to improvements and expansion of your existing product line as well as your hopes for increasing your market share and sales.

The Industry

Chief Characteristics

Describe the industry your company is in. Discuss the industry's profile, including size, geographical dispersion, market, history summation, current status, and total sales and profits for each of the last three years.

The Participants

Discuss the competition and other players (suppliers, wholesalers, distributors, etc.) within your industry. Summarize each participant along a spectrum of weakest to strongest. Briefly discuss the participants' product/service lines and market niche. Discuss more thoroughly the participants with whom you will have direct involvement or competition.

Analyst Summaries

Provide a series of quotes and statements that summarize significant facts, figures, and trends about the industry from various reputable sources. Make sure you properly credit the source and provide the date of publication. Use quotes and statements from diverse sources i.e., industry magazines and newspaper articles. Quotes from personal interviews can also have a powerful impact. These statements should clarify where the industry is headed and the various markets to be served within the industry.

Trends

Discuss where your industry is headed. State whether it is declining, improving, or holding steady and what opportunities there may be. Discuss where it might be in five to 10 years and your relative position within it. Discuss the future of the industry in terms of market need and/or acceptance and profit potential. Describe significant events or changes within the industry that will affect your business positively or negatively.

Common Mistakes to Avoid

- Including too much detail and personal opinion about the company and not enough on significant milestones and potential

- Failing to demonstrate a well-rounded knowledge of major industry players and their potential influence on the company

- Appearing to be a fly-by-night operation

- Evidencing lack of direction and commitment

- Demonstrating poor or inadequate knowledge of the industry and trends

Module 4—Product and Related Services

Suggested Length   1–3 pages

Objective   To describe the product and related services, special features, benefits, and future development plans.

Pertinent Questions

1. What is the purpose of the product/services?

_____

_____

_____

Does the product solve a problem or address an opportunity?

_____

_____

_____

Is it a luxury item or a necessary item?

_____

_____

_____

2. How does the product achieve this purpose?

_____

_____

_____

3. What are its unique features (cost, design, quality, capabilities, etc.)?

_____

_____

_____

_____

4. What is its technological life?

_____

_____

How does it compare with the state of the art?

_____

_____

What is its susceptibility to obsolescence?

_____

_____

To change in style or fashion?

_____

_____

5. What stage of development is the product in? (Check and describe.)
   - ☐ idea
   - ☐ model
   - ☐ working prototype
   - ☐ small production runs
   - ☐ full manufacturing/production (at what level?)
   - ☐ engineering prototype
   - ☐ production prototype

_____

_____

_____

_____

6. How will the product be produced?

_____

_____

_____

Is it capital-intensive?

_____

_____

Is it labor-intensive?

_____

_____

Is it material-intensive?

_____

_____

7. Will all or some of the production be subcontracted?

_____

_____

_____

8. Is this an end-use item or a component of another product?

_____

_____

Does your company's survival depend on someone else?

_____

_____

_____

9. Can your product be protected by patent, copyright, trademark, or service mark? What production will be provided?

_____

_____

10. Do you interface with important noncompetitive equipment whose manufacturer might be reluctant to support your product due to warranty, liability, or image considerations?

_____

_____

_____

11. What new products (spin-offs) do you plan to develop to meet changing market needs, in this industry or others?

_____

_____

_____

12. What are the regulatory or approval requirements from government agencies or other industry participants?

_____

_____

_____

_____

13. Is the product dependent on any natural, industry, or market life cycle? What cycle? (Check and describe.)

☐ introduction

☐ growth

☐ maturity

_____

_____

_____

_____

14. What are the liabilities this product may pose?

_____

_____

_____

What are the insurance requirements?

_____

_____

15. What kind of engineering studies, testing, and evaluation has the product undergone?

_____

_____

_____

16. If more than one product is involved, how will the manufacture and/or promotion of one affect the other?

_____

_____

_____

17. How does this product compare to similar products of competitors?

_____

_____

_____

_____

18. What are any special manufacturing or technological considerations?

_____

_____

_____

What are the maintenance/updating requirements?

_____

_____

_____

19. If equipment is involved, what is its reliability factor?

_____

_____

What is its downtime?

_____

20. What are the related services you will provide?

_____

_____

_____

How will they enhance and increase the profitability of the venture?

_____

_____

_____

Subheadings to Include

Description of Product/Service
Description of the Facilities
Proprietary Features
Future Development Plans
Product Liability

What to Accomplish

In layman's language, explain your product and related services, what they do (that's special or different), and whom they serve. Briefly highlight future plans for improvements or for introducing new products/services.

The following is a suggested sequence of presentation.

Description of Product/Service

Describe exactly what your product/service is and for what it was designed. Discuss how it works, special features, capabilities, and resulting benefits (economic, social, environmental, leisure, etc.). If more than one service or product line is involved, discuss them and how they function together and/or affect each other. State what stage of development the product/service is in.

Description of the Facilities

If the facilities are a focus and part of the product or service (such as a hotel would be), describe them in this section. If the facilities are an adjunct, rather than interrelated with the product or service (such as a machine manufacturing and assembly plant), it would be best to describe them along with the operations description in Module 9.

Describe the facilities and why they are unique or better, i.e., none other like them, more attractive, better proximity to customer base, offer more, etc. Discuss location and why it is advantageous. State what percentage of the facilities is used for revenue-producing services, operations, storage, etc.

Proprietary Features

Discuss any patents, copyrights, trademarks, service marks, or other legally binding agreements that protect your product or service. State if a patent is pending. Overall, discuss how you intend to protect the integrity, confidentiality, and competitive nature of your product and services. Briefly mention any regulatory or approval requirements your product or service must meet. State who has jurisdiction and how you will satisfy these requirements.

Future Development Plans

Describe the nature and application of future development plans. Discuss whether these plans are improvements, an extension of the current product/service line, or plans for other products/services. State whether these plans will address your current market or other markets. Discuss the time frames for these plans. Justify why these plans are important by showing increased or newly generated profits.

Product Liability

Discuss the liability and insurance considerations that are inherent in manufacturing and/or marketing the product. Describe how you plan to limit the company's liability. Provide an estimate of the percent cost of the product that will be applied toward liability coverage.

Common Mistakes to Avoid

- Describing the product/service too technically, too broadly, or too ambiguously

- Failing to identify new, unique, or better capabilities, features, or benefits

- Failing to do the homework on protection availability or not showing how to protect product/service from liability or competition

- Identifying too much red tape and too many uncertainties from regulatory agencies

- Including weak future development plans for improvements, expansion, and staying ahead of market needs and competition

- Failing to consider the reliability, maintenance, and/or updating factors to keep downtime at a minimum

- Failing to include a third-party evaluation of your product/service

Module 5—Technology: Research and Development

Suggested Length	1–2 pages
Objective	To provide an overview of the unique technology your product utilizes. To outline the research and development phase and significant accomplishments.

Note: This module is primarily for ventures that underwent or are continuing to undergo an extensive R&D phase.

Pertinent Questions

1. When did you begin developing the product?

   _____

   _____

   _____

2. Where and under what conditions was research and development conducted?

   _____

   _____

   _____

   Under what supervision?

   _____

   _____

3. How many man-hours are involved?

   _____

4. What instrumentation, chemicals, components, etc., are utilized in the product?

   _____

   _____

   _____

5. What are the costs (to date) to develop the product?

_____

_____

_____

How have you financed these costs?

_____

_____

_____

6. How much of the product is developed? (Check and describe.)
   ☐ electronics
   ☐ mechanics
   ☐ casing
   ☐ packaging/aesthetics
   ☐ full working prototype (how many?)

_____

_____

_____

_____

7. Has the product undergone stress tests, safety tests, and other reliability tests?

_____

_____

8. Have you applied for or received patent protection?

_____

_____

9. What are the regulatory requirements to manufacture, license, or market the product?

_____

_____

_____

10. Do you plan to manufacture this product yourself or license it to an existing manufacturer?

_____

_____

11. How does the technology compare to similar products?

_____

_____

_____

Is it state-of-the-art?

_____

_____

More advanced than competitors?

_____

_____

12. When will research and development be completed?

_____

When will the product be ready for mass production?

_____

When will the product be ready to be marketed and distributed?

_____

What R&D still needs to be done?

_____

_____

13. What contacts have you made concerning the research and development of this product?

_____

_____

Results? (Check and describe.)
☐ potential customers
☐ government agencies
☐ potential manufacturers, distributors
☐ potential investors

_____

_____

14. Who owns the concept, drawings, materials, marketing rights, etc.?

_____

_____

Give a breakdown of each and percent of ownership.

_____

_____

_____

15. What have you learned through R&D?

_____

_____

_____

☐ technology transfer to other applications

_____

_____

☐ spin-off products

_____

_____

16. Have you tested the product in the marketplace? (Check and describe.)
    ☐ ease of use, adaptability
    ☐ user acceptance
    ☐ instructions, training needed

_____

_____

_____

17. What have been the primary accomplishments and breakthroughs?

_____

_____

_____

18. What have been the major risks, problems, and setbacks?

_____

_____

_____

Subheadings to Include

Concept Development
Research, Testing, and Evaluation
Major Milestones and Breakthroughs
Current Status and Continuing R&D

What to Accomplish

Describe how the idea came about. Discuss how you developed the product from the idea stage through to a viable business opportunity. Highlight what you learned in the process and what still needs to be done to move the product into the marketplace.

The following is a suggested sequence of presentation:

Concept Development

Describe how the product came about. Discuss how long it has been in development and the related cost factors. Describe the initial concept and how it has changed and improved through the development process. Discuss any new applications or opportunities that have resulted. State who owns what portion of the concept and/ or product and give the percentages of each. Describe the technology employed in development.

Research, Testing, and Evaluation

Describe all related research, testing, and evaluation activities. Mention any surveys, articles, or studies that may have been published as a result of these activities. Present your findings as factual conclusions and document them as supporting materials in your appendix. State what makes the product reliable. Discuss the results of your research in terms of production needs, cost factors, time requirements, documentation, maintenance, and updating requirements. Describe the facilities, conditions, instrumentation, and supervision with which the research was conducted.

Major Milestones and Breakthroughs

Discuss the significant milestones and accomplishments that were achieved during R&D. State when and under what circumstances the breakthroughs happened. Describe what impact they had or will have on the venture. Discuss how the technology or process is different from or superior to similar products. Describe what risks and problems were overcome to reach these milestones.

Current Status and Continuing R&D

Discuss where the project stands now. Describe how much of the product has been developed and what still needs to be done to protect, manufacture, license, market, and/or distribute it. Discuss how much of this you will be involved in or who may take over the development of these things. State when R&D will be completed. Discuss what contacts you have made regarding the product and the results of the contacts.

**Common Mistakes
to Avoid**

- Investigating or developing superficially; overlooking or not recognizing fundamental problems or flaws

- Testing inadequately; not fully evaluating potential shortcomings or failures by not developing adequate test procedures and conditions

- Failing to obtain certified tests where applicable; trying to establish credibility of results with insufficient data and standards

- Failing to consider safety adequately—shielding, isolation, grounding, types of materials used, etc.

- Paying insufficient attention to reliability factors; failing to define, test, and evaluate reliability considerations

- Failing to plan for future development and manufacturing; inadequately considering manufacturing requirements and materials; failing to include drawings and specifications

- Overdesigning; failing to observe the KIS (Keep It Simple) Principle

- Comparing technology you are currently developing with the technology the competition has now, even though you won't have it on the market for a year or two (the competition's technology and advances will have changed by then)

Module 6—Market Analysis

Suggested Length   3–5 pages

Objective   To demonstrate that you understand the market, that you can penetrate it, and that you are in control of the critical success factors that will enable the company to reach its sales goals. Above all, to prove there is a demand for your product/service.

Pertinent Questions   1. Who or what is your target market? (Check and describe.)

☐ individuals

☐ companies (small, medium, large)

☐ government agencies

☐ other _____

_____

_____

_____

_____

2. What is the size of your target market?

_____

_____

3. Can this market be segmented (by geography, by industries, etc.)? How?

_____

_____

_____

_____

4. What is the profile of your targeted customers?

age _____

sex _____

profession _____

income _____

geographic location _____

other demographics _____

_____

_____

_____

_____

5. What are the major applications of your product or service?

_____

_____

_____

_____

6. For each major application, what are the requirements by customers?

_____

_____

_____

What are the requirements of regulatory agencies?

_____

_____

What are the current ways of filling these requirements?

_____

_____

What are the buying habits of the customers?

_____

_____

_____

7. What will be the impact (economic or otherwise) on the customers who use your product or service?

_____

_____

_____

How much will they save?

_____

_____

What is their return on investment (benefits)?

_____

_____

Will they have to change their ways of doing things?

_____

_____

_____

Will they have to purchase other goods and services to utilize yours?

_____

_____

Will they change their work habits?

_____

_____

Overall, how will you satisfy their needs or wants better?

_____

_____

_____

_____

8. What share of the market do you hope to capture?

_____

_____

9. What is the growth (historical and potential) of your market?

_____

_____

What are the market trends?

_____

_____

_____

_____

Is the market seasonal?

_____

_____

_____

_____

What factors will affect it (economic, government regulation, etc.)?

_____

_____

_____

10. What are your market share objectives for the total available market?

_____

What are your market share objectives for the service available market?

_____

What are your market share objectives for the replacement market?

_____

11. What are your rationale and costs of achieving different levels of penetration?

_____

_____

_____

_____

12. How will you maintain and increase your market share?

_____

_____

_____

_____

How will you satisfy current customer needs?

_____

_____

_____

_____

How will you attract new customers?

_____

_____

_____

_____

How will you offer something new, better, or unique?

_____

_____

_____

_____

13. How will the segments and applications of your market change over the next 3–5 years?

_____

_____

_____

_____

14. Are your products/services bought by others to service their customers?

_____

_____

How does their industry look? What kind of business are they doing?

_____

_____

_____

15. How will you distribute your product? (Check and describe.)

☐ direct

☐ dealer network

☐ wholesale

☐ retail

☐ manufacturer's representatives

☐ other _____

_____

_____

_____

_____

Will it be distributed under your name or someone else's?

_____

_____

16. If transportation is involved, what are the implications of exporting? importing? taxes? tariffs? duties? barriers? foreign exchange and other concerns?

_____

_____

_____

_____

17. Have you received reactions from prospective customers?

_____

What was their reaction?

_____

_____

Have they tested a realistic prototype?

_____

_____

18. Are your sales expectations in line with the manufacturing ability to produce it?

_____

_____

19. Are your pricing, service, and warranty policies attractive and competitive in the marketplace?

_____

_____

20. What does each product/service cost you to sell?

_____

_____

What does each product/service cost you to produce?

_____

_____

_____

21. What have (will) your profits been (be) by product/service?

_____

_____

_____

22. What are your current sales goals by product/service?

_____

_____

What are your current goals by number of units?

_____

_____

What is your sales volume in dollars?

_____

_____

_____

_____

_____

Subheadings to Include	Target Market and Characteristics Analyst Summaries Market Share, Trends, and Growth Potential Sales, Distribution, and Profits by Product/Service Service and Warranty Policies

What to Accomplish
Citing facts from your research and experience, show why and how your company will be successful. Most importantly, prove that there is a market for your product/service and that your potential share and resulting profit projections are realistic.

The following is a suggested sequence of presentation:

Target Market and Characteristics

Describe your target market and who or what it includes; give a profile. Discuss how your product/service meets the needs/wants of this market. Discuss the buying record and habits of your customers. State pertinent facts concerning the size, age, location/area, profession, income, and other demographic information about the market. Allude to any self-performed or professional research, studies, or surveys conducted. Include a list of these in a bibliography in your Appendixes.

Analyst Summaries

Provide a series of quotes and statements that summarize significant facts, figures, and trends about the *market* (and market potential) from various reputable sources. Make sure you properly credit the source and provide the date of publication. The objective is to pinpoint specific market opportunities that exist within the industry and how your product/service capitalizes on these opportunities. The quotes and statements should make it clear what problems and needs exist in your market. It should become evident to the reader that your product/service can solve these problems and/or meet these needs better than existing methods.

Market Share, Trends, and Growth Potential

State the percent share of the market you now have or hope to gain. Discuss the trends of the market—industrywide, regional, and local. State if the market is seasonal, delineate the time frames, and discuss how you will adjust and compensate during the off-season. Discuss how the market may change over the next three to five years. Discuss the growth potential of the entire market and your increased share. State on what assumptions you base these growth patterns (i.e., technology development, changing customer needs, costs, etc.). Discuss your rationale and the costs and risks associated with achieving higher levels of penetration.

Sales, Distribution, and Profits by Product/Service

Discuss your projected sales record by product/service. State what each product/service costs you to produce, distribute, and sell. Discuss how your product/service will be distributed and sold. Describe any unique features of your sales and distribution network. Discuss the implications of transportation, tariffs, duties, foreign exchange, and other government regulations.

Service and Warranty Policies

Are they needed? Will they help you to sell your product(s)? What is normal practice in your industry?

Common Mistakes to Avoid

- Believing that the size of the market (customer) base is equally distributed (for example, your total market may be North Dakota, but the majority of your sales may come from the eastern part of the state)

- Failing to prove that your target market represents the major portion of the demand for your product/service (80/20 rule—20% of the customers may represent 80% of the demand)

- Making unrealistic market share projections (believing you can capture 100% of the market)

- Failing to demonstrate a clear understanding of the product/service to be sold and to what market

- Failing to include an accurate estimate of the profitability of each product/service

- Basing sales projections on a higher degree of output than you have adequately demonstrated can actually be met

- Establishing pricing that is not in line with target market needs, desires, or ability to pay

- Not properly assessing the total market potential or changes in the market caused by economic, social, or other trends

- Not supporting your target market assumptions in light of advances in technology, government regulations, population shifts, and economic forces (oil prices, interest rates, etc.)

- Addressing (attacking) your market universally; not segmenting your market into various components and developing profiles of each; defining your market too broadly

- Presenting your facts to make your market appear subservient to your company's needs instead of vice versa

Module 7—Competitive Analysis

Suggested Length   2-3 pages

Objective   To show that you are fully aware of the competitive forces at work in your marketplace. To explain your strengths over the competition and how you will counteract their advantages and overcome or compensate for your weaknesses.

Pertinent Questions   1. Who are your nearest and largest major competitors?

_____

_____

_____

_____

2. Is their business steady, increasing, or decreasing?

_____

_____

_____

Why?

_____

_____

_____

3. How does your business compare to your competitors' (strengths and weaknesses of each)?

☐ in length of time in business?

☐ in sales volume (units and dollars)?

☐ in size and number of employees, suppliers, and support personnel?

☐ in number of customers? share of market? product niche?

_____

_____

_____

_____

4. What are the similarities/dissimilarities between your business and your competitors' business?

_____

_____

_____

_____

5. On what basis will you compete with them? (Check and describe.)

☐ product superiority

☐ price

☐ advertising

☐ technology/innovation

☐ other _____

_____

_____

_____

_____

6. In what aspect(s) is your business better? (What is your distinctive competence?) (Check and describe.)

☐ operations

☐ management

☐ product

☐ price

☐ service

☐ delivery

☐ other _____

_____

_____

_____

_____

7. What have you learned by observing your competition?

_____

_____

_____

_____

8. What competition will you meet in each product/service line?

_____

_____

_____

_____

9. How does your product/service compare with the competition in the eyes of customers?

_____

_____

_____

_____

10. What do you know about others like you who are not yet in the market?

_____

_____

_____

11. If you have no competition, what kind (whom) might you create by being successful in the marketplace?

_____

_____

_____

12. Do you threaten the major strategic objectives or self-image of the competition?

_____

_____

Will you seriously affect their profits? (Will they attempt to destroy you at any cost?)

_____

_____

_____

Subheadings to Include   Competitors' Profile
                                      Product/Service Comparison
                                      Market Niche and Share
                                      Comparison of Strengths and Weaknesses

What to Accomplish   Give a brief rundown on the other industry participants. Highlight your particular competitive edge.

The following is a suggested sequence of presentation:

Competitors' Profile

Discuss the competition: size, age, locations, sales volume, management, mode of operation, and other characteristics. Discuss potential competitors who may enter your market.

Product/Service Comparison

Discuss the similarities and differences between your product/service and that of the competition. Compare your operations and management style with those of your various competitors. Highlight whatever it is that makes your product/service and company more attractive in the marketplace.

Market Niche and Share

State the approximate percentage each of your competitors holds in the market. Discuss those that hold the large percentages and why they have an edge. Discuss the competitors who have come or are coming on strong and are making (or expected to make) bigger gains in the market. Discuss the particular segments of the market that each of your competitors addresses. Discuss your niche in relation to these and what percent of the total market it makes up. Describe where the market is headed and how each competitor's niche and share may change over the next three to five years.

Comparison of Strengths and Weaknesses

Discuss your strengths and weaknesses in relation to your major competitors. It is helpful to list the variables down the left-hand column and the competition and your company along the top of the page. The reader can quickly summarize the characteristics, as well as the strengths and weaknesses, of all participants at a glance. The major strengths and weaknesses you should summarize are product superiority, price advantages, market advantages (large contracts with customers or suppliers, proximity to a larger market, proximity of labor supplies, raw materials, energy, transportation, land, or other resources), and management strengths and weaknesses (experience and track record, skills, etc.).

Common Mistakes to Avoid

- Not identifying known major competitors
- Underestimating competitive strength and potential
- Failing to demonstrate your competitive edge—what makes you unique or better
- Having no strategy for counteracting current competition or emerging competition
- Assuming you have no competition
- Failing to show an awareness of competitors' plans in the market and their business cycles.

Module 8—Marketing Strategy

Suggested Length   2–3 pages

Objective   To explain specifically how you will enter the market, obtain a niche, maintain a market share, and achieve the stated financial projections.

Pertinent Questions

1. What is the sales appeal of your product/service?

   _____

   _____

   _____

   What is special or unique about it?

   _____

   _____

   _____

   _____

2. How will you attract and maintain your market?

   _____

   _____

   _____

   _____

   How will you expand it?

   _____

   _____

   _____

   Over what period of time?

   _____

   _____

   _____

3. What are your marketing priorities among segments and applications? (You can't be all things to all people, regardless of the opportunity.)

_____

_____

_____

4. How will you identify prospective customers?

_____

_____

_____

_____

5. How will you reach the decision makers?

_____

_____

_____

_____

6. How will you decide whom to contact?

_____

_____

_____

_____

In what order?

_____

_____

_____

7. What level of selling effort will you implement?

_____

_____

_____

Why is this the best approach?

_____

_____

_____

How many salespeople? In-house staff or manufacturers' representatives?

_____

_____

_____

_____

How much direct mail and brochure distribution?

_____

_____

_____

_____

How many trade shows? Which ones?

_____

_____

_____

_____

8. What advertising/promotion media will you use? (Check and describe.)
   ☐ radio
   ☐ newspaper
   ☐ trade journals
   ☐ magazines
   ☐ television

_____

_____

_____

_____

9. What are your efficiency ratios and conversion rates?

_____

_____

_____

How many calls are made per demonstration?

_____

_____

How many demonstrations per sale?

_____

_____

How much direct mail and expected response rate?

_____

_____

How many other media ads and expected response rate?

_____

_____

10. How long will the activities above take?

_____

_____

_____

11. What will each customer's average order size be?

_____

_____

What kind of repeat orders can you expect?

_____

_____

12. What are the quotas and sales productivity of each salesperson?

_____

_____

_____

What is the commission structure?

_____

_____

What is the sales cycle?

_____

_____

What are the milestones for meeting sales expectations?

_____

_____

_____

13. What geographic areas will be covered?

_____

_____

_____

14. What will your pricing strategy be?

_____

_____

Will your margins be low or high?

_____

_____

_____

What will your discount policy be?

_____

_____

_____

What will your dealer margins be?

_____

_____

_____

15. How may pricing change over time?

_____

_____

How may pricing change after recouping R&D costs?

_____

_____

What about possible pricing wars with competition?

_____

_____

What are the critical supply and demand factors?

_____

_____

_____

16. How will your packaging and labeling enhance name identification and foster brand loyalty? (Why will a prospective customer want to buy your product just by seeing it?)

_____

_____

_____

17. What will your credit and collection policies be?

_____

_____

18. What kind (and level) of service, warranties, and guarantees will you offer?

_____

_____

How will you promote these?

_____

_____

How may these affect profits?

_____

_____

Subheadings to Include

Market Penetration Goals
Pricing and Packaging
Sales and Distribution
Service and Warranty Policies
Advertising, Public Relations, and Promotions

What to Accomplish

Describe your plan of action for being successful in the market. Discuss how your internal policies and your utilization of the media will contribute to that success. Reference your marketing plan if you have developed one independently of the business plan.

The following is a suggested sequence of presentation:

Market Penetration Goals

Describe your plans for entering the market. State what your estimated sales and share will be. Discuss the sales appeal among specific segments of the market. Discuss how you will identify prospective customers within each segment, how you will prioritize them, and how you will reach them. State your timetables for achieving these penetration goals and how your strategy may be affected by the reactions of competitors. Discuss any major customers whom you have precommitted and how they may help you to further penetrate the market.

Pricing and Packaging

Describe your pricing policies and how they are determined. Discuss the influences of the competition, discounts, cost of goods, market forces, and other factors that will affect pricing. Justify your prices, particularly if they are substantially above or below the prices of similar products/services in the marketplace. Above all, demonstrate that your pricing decision is based on your company's ability to make a profit.

Discuss your packaging and labeling design plans. Describe how the brand name, colors, logo, and overall packaging appeal will entice customers to buy. Discuss the directions or instructions that accompany the product and how you make the product easy to use.

Sales and Distribution

Discuss any relationships you have with suppliers and/or distributors. Mention any distribution or licensing agreements that are in force or that you are seeking. Describe how your product/service will be distributed and over what geographical area. Discuss the method(s) of sales and retailing, direct sales, and other methods. Discuss how these will be attracted, compensated, and controlled.

Discuss your selling arrangements in terms of cash sales, financing, leasing, credit, and payment terms. If you will be employing salespeople, discuss their quotas and incentives. (Remember that sales volume will be directly proportional to the number of effective sales calls made. Prospective investors will want to see you knocking on doors.) Discuss briefly your hiring, training, and promotion program.

Service and Warranty Policies

Describe your service arrangements, product support, warranty terms, and customer orientation of these things. Discuss how these policies make you competitive and how they may affect profits. Discuss the procedures for implementing these policies. State how they are reviewed by management and how they may change or be improved on as you gain experience. Describe how you will handle customer complaints and other problems with the product/service.

Advertising, Public Relations, and Promotions

Describe your advertising, public relations, and promotional programs and campaigns. Discuss the media you will use and any professional ad agencies you may retain. Describe your overall approach and strategy for introducing your product/service and gaining it market familiarity and acceptance. Discuss how the company's name or the product/service name may contribute to market identity. Discuss your attendance at conventions and trade shows within the industry.

Common Mistakes to Avoid

■ Discussing marketing and sales in the same terms (*Sales* is dealing directly with your customers; it is a developed art form. *Marketing* is enticing them to consider your product; it is an acquired discipline.)

■ Justifying your prices by the cost to produce, market, and/or sell your product/service (Sales price is a function of value in the eyes of your customers only. Too low a price is as detrimental as too high a price.)

■ Assuming that your sales efforts can be set up with minimal time and expense (It takes as much as one year for a salesperson to get acquainted with a product and learn a territory. Start-up ventures should investigate using an established agent/representative/ distributor network; the learning curve and amount of time it takes to get established are much shorter.)

■ Assuming your distribution network will give your product/service equal sales time if you do use an independent agent or representative

■ Failing to promote marketable differences in your product over the competition

■ Attempting to immediately fill several lucrative but unrelated market gaps

■ Presenting a strategy that is too broad, irrational, or unachievable

■ Underestimating the importance of packaging and brand name

Module 9—Manufacturing Process/Operations

Suggested Length   3–5 pages

Objective   To explain how you will produce your product in a cost-efficient way and ready it for the market.

Pertinent Questions
1. How will you accomplish production (or conduct service operations)?

   _____

   _____

   _____

   _____

2. How much will you do internally?

   _____

   _____

   _____

   By what methods?

   _____

   _____

   _____

3. How much of production will be accomplished through subcontracts?

   _____

   _____

   Initially?

   _____

   _____

   After two or three years?

   _____

   _____

4. What materials and components are required for production?

_____

_____

What are the critical parts?

_____

_____

5. Who/what are the sources of supply for these parts?

_____

_____

Are any of these parts sole-sourced?

_____

_____

Do you have backup vendors or alternatives should materials or suppliers become unavailable?

_____

_____

What are the lead times of these parts?

_____

_____

6. Are production facilities and equipment leased or purchased?

_____

_____

What is the condition of the facilities and equipment?

_____

_____

Are there any liens on the property or equipment?

_____

Have you done a title search?

_____

7. What is your planned capacity for level of production or operations?

   _____

   _____

   In dollars? _____

   In units? _____

   How may this be expanded?

   _____

   _____

   What are the production cycles?

   _____

   _____

   _____

8. What are the standard costs for production at different volume levels (breakdown of fixed and variable costs)?

   _____

   _____

   _____

9. What are your plans for equipment setup and facility layout so production flows with a minimum of problems and bottlenecks?

   _____

   _____

   _____

10. In planning facility and equipment layout, have you considered:

    future expansion needs/plans?

    _____

    _____

    output capacity—will it meet peak demand or meet lower levels of demand and stockpiled inventory?

    _____

    _____

space requirements for rest rooms, office, storage, receiving, manufacturing, lounge, other?

_____

_____

11. Will the plant be set up for process layout (machines grouped by function) or production layout (machines grouped according to the needs of the product being manufactured)?

_____

_____

_____

12. Have you determined the order in which jobs will be done at each workstation? (Check and describe.)

☐ first come, first served

☐ shortest operation time (SOT), first served

☐ last in, first served

☐ other _____

_____

_____

_____

_____

13. Have you separated the cost to produce each unit by material and labor?

_____

_____

Have you figured the indirect costs, i.e., supplies, utilities, management and clerical salaries, insurance, taxes, depreciation, interest, etc.?

_____

_____

_____

What is the break-even point?

_____

_____

_____

_____

14. What are your other production control procedures?

_____

_____

_____

What are your safety record and procedures?

_____

_____

_____

15. What is your quality control system?

_____

_____

_____

_____

_____

16. What are your inventory control considerations?

_____

_____

_____

What is your level of "buffer stock" needed to absorb random variations in demand?

_____

_____

_____

What kind of fixed-order or cycle-order inventory system will you implement?

_____

_____

_____

What is the shelf life of the product?

_____

_____

_____

17. What are your labor considerations?

    _____

    _____

    _____

    What are the effects of possible strikes/union activity?

    _____

    _____

    _____

    What are the training needs?

    _____

    _____

    _____

    What are the effects of changes in compensation/productivity, structure, or quotas?

    _____

    _____

    _____

18. How will you make the most effective use of your labor pool?

    _____

    _____

    _____

    Can your personnel handle more than one machine or function?

    _____

    _____

19. What is the potential environmental impact of your plant location or manufacturing process, in terms of:

    restrictions? licenses? zoning? _____

    disposal of waste? _____

    pollution and noise control? _____

    other considerations? _____

    _____

    _____

    _____

    _____

20. What are the advantages and disadvantages of your present or planned location, in terms of:

    proximity to customers? _____

    proximity to labor, suppliers, capital? _____

    access to transportation, energy, utilities (rates), and other resources? _____

    state and local laws (zoning, regulation, etc.) _____

21. What are the characteristics of your location in terms of size?

    _____

    _____

    _____

    What are the characteristics of your location in terms of structure?

    _____

    _____

    _____

    What are the characteristics of your location in terms of surroundings (is the area stable, changing, improving, deteriorating)?

    _____

    _____

    _____

22. What short-term or long-range plans do you have/need for the facility and location?

    _____

    _____

    _____

    What short-term or long-range plans do you have/need for renovations and costs?

    _____

    _____

    _____

    What short-term or long-range plans do you have/need for additional features or replacement fixtures?

    _____

    _____

What short-term or long-range plans do you have/need for a new location?

_____

_____

_____

23. How does your location affect your operating costs?

_____

_____

_____

24. What other businesses (kinds?) are in the area?

_____

_____

_____

_____

25. What will be the costs and timing of any acquisitions?

_____

_____

_____

_____

26. Overall, what production or operating advantages do you have?

_____

_____

_____

_____

27. What economic impact may your plant location, and business in general, have on the community in which you will be located? (Check and describe.)

☐ creating jobs

☐ improving the sales of area suppliers

☐ spurring existing companies to relocate to the area or spurring new companies

☐ other _____

_____

_____

_____

Subheadings to Include

Location
Facilities and Equipment
Manufacturing Process and Operations
Labor Considerations
Environmental and Economic Impact

What to Accomplish

Demonstrate you have a good handle on all aspects of your company's manufacturing process and operations. This is where most business plans fall short, because it is the area that causes most businesses to fail. It is in this area that the major costs and headaches of a company are found. You want to show you have given these issues serious thought. Describe how you will minimize the cost and inherent problems of manufacturing while maximizing profits through efficient operations.

The following is a suggested sequence of presentation:

Location

Describe your company's location or proposed location. State if the land will be purchased, leased, or rented. Describe the surrounding area and other types of businesses in the neighborhood. Discuss the advantages and disadvantages of your location in terms of proximity to customers or markets; availability of labor, suppliers, and capital; access to transportation, energy, utilities, and other resources. Discuss the state and local laws such as zoning, licenses, and other regulations that may affect your company. Highlight the favorable climate that exists in and around the location. Discuss how your location will affect your operating costs. Finally, state whether your long-range plans and needs call for you to remain where you are or move to establish a new location.

Facilities and Equipment

Describe the characteristics of the facilities in terms of size, structure, and condition. Describe the kind of equipment used in your manufacturing operations and its condition. State whether the facilities and equipment are purchased, leased, or rented. Discuss any special parts or needs that must accompany the facilities and equipment. Discuss the maintenance and replacement requirements of the facilities and equipment. Highlight how and why the facilities and equipment give you better production or operating advantages over similar businesses. Finally, discuss the long-range needs and plans for your facilities and equipment.

Manufacturing Process and Operations

Describe how you will manufacture and produce your product and/or conduct service operations. Discuss the methods and processes involved. State how much of this will be done internally and how much will be subcontracted. Discuss how internal operations or subcontracting relationships may change over the next few years. Describe the raw materials and/or components used in producing your product. Discuss how these are supplied and what your backup system is should your primary suppliers become unavailable.

State your current or initial projected capacity for level of production or operations in dollars and in units. Discuss how this may be expanded or changed in any other way. Break down the fixed and variable costs of production and operations at different volume levels. Describe the costs to produce each unit by material and labor. Include the indirect costs (utilities, taxes, insurance, etc.) and show the break-even point.

Describe the product/operations layout (a sample is included in this guide's Appendix). Discuss work flow and production control procedures. Discuss your safety program, quality control system, and inventory control system. Show how they are conducive to a positive and productive work environment and are cost-effective as well.

Labor Considerations

Discuss what labor requirements you will have and how you will hire and train personnel. Discuss how you will handle the possibility of strikes and other labor union activities. Discuss how you will minimize turnovers and structure compensation, productivity quotas, and employee benefits. Discuss how you will handle discipline cases and how you will communicate company policies as they relate to infractions and expectations.

Environmental and Economic Impact

Describe how your company and its manufacturing operations will affect the environment and the community. Discuss how you will dispose of waste, apply for applicable licenses, and be affected by other restrictions, such as pollution and noise control. Highlight the economic benefits that will result from your business's operating in the community. Discuss the "trickle down" effect of your business boosting others, creating jobs, etc.

Common Mistakes to Avoid

■ Failing to properly assess the manufacturing process, operations, and alternative methods in terms of their costs (taxes, freight, installation, maintenance, etc.), production capabilities, serviceability, delivery times, and other considerations

■ Not adequately identifying or providing for ancillary needs and equipment, such as special drainage requirement, ventilation systems, fixtures, etc.

■ Planning improperly for efficient plant layout, materials handling, work spaces, travel, and other considerations

■ Poorly scheduling work force, hiring and layoff, overtime, additional shifts, subcontracting, and inventories

■ Not optimizing the combination of available capacities to meet demand and hold down costs

■ Demonstrating poor inventory control planning; establishing no balance between meeting customer demand and minimizing associated costs, i.e., ordering production, handling and storage, capital allocations, shortages, etc.

■ Failing to maintain proper inventory levels; having an inadequate inventory control system or inadequate controls in monitoring the purchasing function

■ Failing to identify and account for all product costs (fixed, variable, indirect)

■ Exhibiting poor personnel management and hiring practices; paying insufficient attention to selection process, training, pay scales and benefits, union influences, and explanation of company policies and expectations

■ Underestimating the economic and environmental (especially as it pertains to regulation) impact

■ Failing to plan for long-range needs and changes in location, facility, and equipment

Module 10—Management and Ownership

Suggested Length   2-3 pages

Objective   To demonstrate that the management and leadership are capable, fairly compensated, and given every incentive to be successful. To show the ownership distribution, who the owners are, and how much they own.

Pertinent Questions

1. Who are your key managers?

   _____

   _____

   _____

   _____

2. What is the personal history of each principal?

   age _____

   _____

   _____

   educational background (formal and informal) _____

   _____

   _____

   talents, skills, abilities _____

   _____

   _____

   health _____

   _____

   outside interests _____

   _____

   _____

3. What does each principal bring to this venture?

   number of years of direct experience in industry _____

   track record _____

   length of time with this project _____

   business management background _____

   _____

4. What is the position and role of each principal?

    title _____

    responsibilities, duties, and/or overlapping functions _____

    _____

5. What is the compensation package of each principal?

    salary _____

    profit sharing _____

    bonuses and other fringe benefits _____

    terms of employment _____

    _____

6. What is the ownership interest of each principal?

    _____

    _____

    _____

    _____

7. Who is on the board of directors?

    inside representation _____

    outside representation _____

    age _____

    corporate affiliation _____

    compensation _____

    ownership _____

    special contributions _____

8. What is the primary objective of the current owners and managers? (Check and describe.)

☐ sell out in x number of years

☐ buy out investors

☐ license idea for royalties

☐ franchise idea

☐ other _____

_____

_____

_____

_____

_____

_____

_____

9. How do you intend to attract and compensate additional key people as the company grows?

_____

_____

_____

_____

10. Do any of your people have outstanding "noncompete" agreements with previous employers?

_____

_____

Do they have one with you?

_____

_____

Have you obtained legal advice on their validity and applicability?

_____

_____

_____

11. Has the loss of a key member of your team been considered from a tax-planning standpoint, from a knowledge, information and learning curve perspective, and from a management succession point of view?

_____

_____

_____

12. Is there a written succession plan?

_____

_____

13. How much life insurance is being carried on key personnel in which the company is the beneficiary?

_____

_____

_____

14. What is the amount of stock currently authorized and issued?

_____

_____

15. Who are your current stockholders?

_____

_____

_____

_____

How many shares does each own?

_____

_____

_____

What are the warrants, rights, options?

_____

_____

_____

16. What about you?

    What is your reason for going into business?

    _____

    _____

    _____

    _____

    Are you physically suited to do the job?

    _____

    _____

    _____

17. Who is on your professional team? (Check and describe.)

    ☐ lawyer

    ☐ accountant

    ☐ banker

    ☐ tax specialist

    ☐ trade association

    ☐ consultants (marketing, management, systems, etc.)

    _____

    _____

    _____

    _____

Subheadings to Include

Management
Board of Directors
Ownership
Professional Support Resources

What to Accomplish

Show that your company has proper balance. Having too many marketing and sales types of people in management is as bad as having too many bean counters (finance people) making the critical decisions. Demonstrate adequate expertise in all areas of marketing, management, technical finance, manufacturing, etc. Show you have recruited in the areas where you personally are weak. Above all, differentiate between ownership and management roles, even if they are assumed by the same individuals.

The following is a suggested sequence of presentation:

Management

Discuss your management team. Give a brief background of the principals (decision makers). Describe each principal's distinctive competence and what each brings to the company. Discuss education, experience, knowledge of industry, special talents, training, skills, and abilities.

Discuss the principals' position, duties, and responsibilities. State how long they have been with the project and any significant accomplishments with the company; Discuss each principal's compensation package, i.e., salary, profit sharing, bonuses and incentives, fringe benefits, and other terms of employment. State what the principals' objectives with the company are, i.e., what they want to get out of their involvement, short-term or long-range. Discuss any noncompete agreements or other legal contracts that each has executed with the company.

If all the management positions have not yet been filled, describe the qualifications that a person will need to fill these positions. State how and when you expect to recruit additional key people. Discuss how you intend to attract and compensate them. Along these lines, describe any positions that may be created as your company grows.

Describe what options or alternatives you may pursue if you lose a key person. State what your own personal plans are for grooming a successor. Discuss how you will minimize the negative impacts of losing or having to fire key managers.

Allude to the résumés and personal references from customers, suppliers, bankers, former employers, etc., on each of your key people that are included as supporting documents in your plan's appendix.

Board of Directors

Discuss who is on your board of directors and why they are valuable to the business. State what their field of expertise is and their other corporate affiliations. Describe any special contributions they have already made or are expected to make. State how the board members are compensated for their time and advice, how often they meet, and how much control or influence they wield.

If you have not yet recruited a board of directors, describe the kind of individuals you would like to place and how and when you expect to recruit them.

Ownership

Give a breakdown of the ownership interest of all parties—who owns what and how much. Describe the form of ownership, i.e., stock, partnership percentages, notes, etc. State the type of ownership, i.e., preferred stock, common stock, straight debt, debt with warrants, convertible debentures, etc.

Discuss the amount and kind of ownership in reserve (not yet issued). Discuss how the ownership breakdown may change by taking on additional managers and/or capital from investors. Describe the proposed distribution of ownership if not yet firm.

Discuss any plans or agreements you have pertaining to buyouts, dissolution of company, managers/owners leaving the company, and other possible developments. Discuss the warrants, privileges, rights, and options of all current and future owners.

If you are seeking financing through this business plan, allude to personal financial statements included in your Appendix.

Professional Support Resources

Describe your support team and how each member has assisted or will assist in the development and ongoing management of your company. A partial list may include lawyer, accountant, banker, tax specialist, trade association affiliation, public relations consultant, marketing/advertising consultant, technical/systems consultant, etc.

If you have not yet used consultants, show the reader you are aware of the support services your company may need. Discuss which professional you may use and when he or she would come into play.

Common Mistakes to Avoid

- Having friends, relatives, or other people in key management positions who are not qualified for specialized functions

- Wanting the reader to assume that a successful manager from a different industry will be successful in your company's industry

- Failing to protect the proprietary nature of your product or confidentiality of your operations by not having key people sign noncompete agreements and/or employment contracts

- Offering particular people too much ownership or other compensation because you are desperate to attract and keep good people (base your incentives on achieving milestones so that key people will pay for themselves)

- Failing to identify and recruit a prestigious and active board of directors

- Demonstrating an unwillingness to step aside after the company outgrows your entrepreneurial inspiration and requires more of a maintenance-type manager

- Not having a succession plan or crisis management plan in the event of unexpectedly losing key people

- Failing to provide for reserve ownership for use in second-round financing, attracting additional board members or management, with a minimum of hassle from current owners

- Locking into wrong-type ownership, in light of tax benefits, dividend disbursement, or other priorities of current or future owners

- Failing to provide for advice, counsel, and support services of needed professionals

Module 11—Administration, Organization, and Personnel

Suggested Length   1-2 pages

Objective   To show control and efficiency of standard administrative functions. To outline the company organization, lines of authority, and responsibility. To give a sketch of your staffing needs.

Pertinent Questions

1. What is your organizational structure? (Include an organization chart.)

_____

_____

_____

Does everyone know who reports/answers to whom?

_____

_____

_____

Are clear lines of authority and responsibility established?

_____

_____

2. Do you have a bookkeeping system set up?

_____

_____

_____

3. What are your administrative policies, procedures, and controls for billings, payments, and accounts receivable?

_____

_____

_____

What are your administrative policies, procedures, and controls for management reporting?

_____

_____

_____

What are your administrative policies, procedures, and controls for employee training, probation periods, promotions, incentives, discipline, etc.?

_____

_____

_____

What are your administrative policies, procedures, and controls for travel, phone usage, supplies, car allowance, and other expenses?

_____

_____

_____

4. What are your management philosophies and style?

_____

_____

_____

_____

_____

_____

How will you motivate employees (incentives)?

_____

_____

_____

_____

How will you create a positive work environment?

_____

_____

_____

_____

How will you manage for goal attainment (MBO—Management By Objectives)?

_____

_____

_____

_____

How will you encourage creativity and entrepreneurship?

_____

_____

_____

_____

How will you foster commitment and loyalty in your employees?

_____

_____

_____

_____

5. What is your current (or initially planned) personnel makeup?

   number of employees _____

   skills _____

   seasonal hiring and layoff factors _____

   _____

6. What is your average or expected turnover?

   _____

   _____

   _____

7. What are your personnel needs?

   6 months _____

   1 year _____

   3 years _____

   number of people needed _____

   skills _____

   full-time _____

   part-time _____

   _____

   _____

   _____

8. Are the people you will need (level of knowledge, qualifications) available in the marketplace, or will you have to train?

_____

_____

_____

_____

9. How will you attract and compensate employees? (Check and describe.)

☐ by skill level

☐ by job class

☐ other _____

_____

_____

_____

10. How do your personnel know where they stand?

What are they supposed to do (job descriptions)?

_____

_____

_____

When are they supposed to do it?

_____

_____

_____

How are they supposed to do it?

_____

_____

_____

Expectations of management and prospects for advancement?

_____

_____

_____

_____

_____

11. Do you have periodic performance evaluations?

_____

_____

_____

12. What are the costs of these administrative functions?

_____

_____

_____

_____

Subheadings to Include

Organizational Chart
Administrative Procedures and Controls
Staffing and Training
Management Control Systems

What to Accomplish

Your readers are going to want to know how the company is managed as much as who is managing it. Demonstrate your awareness and understanding of the administrative details. Explain what personnel are needed and how you will fill and train these positions. Include an organization chart that illustrates the company's structure, lines of authority, responsibility, and delegation. Finally, give a brief synopsis of your management style and systems for ensuring excellence.

The following is a suggested sequence of presentation:

Organizational Chart

Illustrate the lines of authority, responsibility, and delegation with a chart. Make it clear who answers to whom. Do not make these areas of accountability look too authoritarian or rigid. Allow for flexibility and overlap of duties if appropriate for your situation. The reader should be able to glance at the chart and get a clear understanding of the management and personnel structure of the company. A sample organizational chart can be found in this guide's Appendix.

Administrative Procedures and Controls

Describe your administrative systems, procedures, and controls. Mention specifically how you will handle the accounting and bookkeeping functions. Discuss how you will monitor and audit customer payments, bills incurred by the company, and accounts receivable. State how you will track and control internal expenses and operating costs. Discuss any other major administrative systems that are a necessary function of your venture, such as ordering, collecting, receiving, organizing, filing, storing, disseminating, and disposing of goods, services, and/or information.

Staffing and Training

Discuss your current or needed personnel and their functions. State how they complement one another. Describe the nature, length, and cost of training needed for employees. Discuss any present or planned employment contracts you expect to utilize and enforce. Describe how personnel are identified, attracted, hired, and compensated. State your current or planned number of employees and future provisions for growth. Describe the learning and experience curve for different positions and the amount of time before personnel can function independently and productively in these positions. Sample job descriptions may be included in your plan's Appendix.

Management Control Systems

Briefly summarize your management philosophies and style. Tie these in with how you will go about getting the most out of your people. Describe your plans to encourage group goals over individual goals. Discuss how you will prevent your team from stagnating or becoming too bogged down in the routine and predictable decisions. In general, discuss how you will keep the lines of communication open, encourage creativity and commitment to company goals, and remain lean, flexible, and action-oriented.

Common Mistakes to Avoid

- Using a poor or inadequate system of accounting and other business records

- Failing to have some preconceived notions on how to manage and encourage the best possible performance

- Not having enough personnel to accomplish the tasks at hand

- Being overstaffed; too many people doing too little work

- Establishing no clear lines of authority or accountability; having poor management control systems

- Planning inadequately for future staff needs in light of growth or other changes

- Adopting poor training and orientation procedures for personnel

- Offering substandard compensation and incentives

- Having top-heavy management (too many chiefs and not enough Indians)

- Failing to demonstrate company purpose and commitment to team goals (not showing that what is good for the whole is good for the parts)

Module 12—Milestones, Schedule, and Strategic Planning

Suggested Length   1–2 pages

Objective   To outline major company objectives and explain how and when they will be achieved.

Pertinent Questions   1. What needs to be done to launch this venture?

_____

_____

_____

_____

What needs to be done to raise the capital?

_____

_____

_____

_____

What needs to be done to identify and penetrate the market?

_____

_____

_____

_____

What needs to be done to identify, recruit, place, and train management and personnel?

_____

_____

_____

_____

_____

_____

What needs to be done to locate the company, line up suppliers, etc.?

_____

_____

_____

_____

What needs to be done to become operational?

_____

_____

_____

_____

2. Who is going to do these things?

_____

_____

_____

_____

When are they expected to be completed?

_____

_____

_____

3. What are the critical milestones and junctures that must be reached to make other things happen?

_____

_____

_____

_____

4. Do you have a "time line" chart that identifies these milestones with month/day/year for completion?

_____

_____

5. Have you done any strategic planning for the venture?

_____

_____

_____

_____

6. What professionals and consultants have you retained, or will be needed, to keep you on schedule and help you reach your goals?

_____

_____

_____

_____

7. Do your goals reflect a "real world" view or hopeful thinking?

_____

_____

_____

Are your goals actually attainable within the time frames you set down?

_____

_____

_____

_____

How will you assure their attainment with a minimal margin of error?

_____

_____

_____

_____

8. What will you do if/when you do not reach key milestones?

_____

_____

_____

_____

9. Do you have a unified and coordinated effort toward the attainment of these goals?

_____

_____

_____

_____

Subheadings to Include

Major Milestones
Schedule
Strategic Planning

What to Accomplish

Demonstrate that you know what must be done and how you will pursue these goals in a realistic way, within a reasonable time frame. Concentrate on the critical or all-important milestones. Summarize the implications of not attaining these milestones and what alternatives you may then pursue. Your goals should be centered around positioning and strengthening yourself in the marketplace through strategic planning.

The following is a suggested sequence of presentation:

Major Milestones

Summarize the significant goals that you and your venture have already reached. Describe how you attained them and what you learned in the process. Discuss what needs to be done and what must happen for you to be successful with the company. State who is in charge of seeing that these things are accomplished. Refer the reader to the time line schedule for when these things are expected to be completed. Describe why these goals and time frames are realistic. Finally, give an example of the teamwork and unified commitment toward the attainment of these goals.

Schedule

Include a time line chart. This chart is a schedule of significant milestones and their priority for completion. The far-left-hand column indicates the day, month, and year for completion. The second column from the left states the milestone or goal to be completed. The third column from the left states who is charged with the task of overseeing or completing the goal. The last column states what options or alternatives may be pursued if the goal is not attained.

There are several ways to present the milestones within the chart. You may list them in order of priority or in order of importance. (The two are not necessarily the same.) You may also list them in logical order for completion. In other words, one must happen before the other can be considered or reached.

A sample time line chart is included in the Appendixes.

Strategic Planning

This is normally a very difficult issue for an owner/manager to tackle. It takes quite a bit of foresight and expertise, combining academic techniques with past experience in the company/industry. As with all other issues in your plan, do not try to bluff or be afraid to admit that you don't have all the answers. Your best bet is to consult professionals in the field. Lacking the resources to get professional help, get together with your partners, managers, staff, friends, and other people involved and conduct a brainstorming session.

In a brainstorming session no idea or comment is too farfetched. Creativity and openness are to be encouraged, without criticism or qualification. Have your team throw out ideas on all major aspects of your product/service and operations. After all ideas are exhausted, prioritize, assign, and begin putting some direction toward their exploration.

You should strategize according to:

■ learning/expertise curve

■ industry participants

■ leadership/management style

■ available resources

■ security of information

■ flexibility, simplicity

■ new approaches, element of surprise

The biggest factor in formulating effective strategies, while avoiding ones with inherent risks and failure, is to have an honest assessment of your strengths and weaknesses and to ask the right questions. In writing this section of your business plan, make it clear to the reader that you are indeed addressing the right questions.

Common Mistakes to Avoid

■ Failing to identify and prioritize the really significant or critical milestones

■ Inadequately describing how you will attain your goals and who is responsible for the task

■ Setting unrealistic milestones, given available resources and/or time frames for completion

■ Failing to offer alternative plans of action if and when major milestones are not reached within a designated time period

■ Failing to look ahead and plan for ways to improve sales and operations

■ Believing that everything will go according to schedule

Module 13—The Critical Risks and Problems

Suggested Length   1-2 pages

Objective   To demonstrate your knowledge of inevitable or potential problems and risks; to show your willingness to face up to them and deal with them in a forthright manner.

Pertinent Questions
1. What are the inherent and potential problems, risks, and other negatives your business will/may be faced with?

_____

_____

_____

_____

_____

_____

_____

_____

_____

_____

_____

_____

_____

_____

2. Is the company or any principal involved in any threatened or pending litigation or disciplinary action?

_____

_____

_____

3. Is the company facing any stringent regulatory requirements?

_____

_____

_____

4. Is the company facing legal liability or other insurance problems?

_____

_____

_____

_____

5. What can you do to avoid these problems?

_____

_____

_____

_____

6. When are they likely to occur?

_____

_____

_____

7. How will you deal with them as they arise?

_____

_____

_____

_____

8. How can you minimize their impact?

_____

_____

_____

_____

9. What can be learned from these problems?

_____

_____

_____

_____

10. How can you possibly turn these problems into opportunities?

_____

_____

_____

_____

Subheadings to Include

Summary of Major Problems Overcome
Inevitable Risks and Problems
Potential Risks and Problems
Worst-Case Scenarios

What to Accomplish

Address the negatives that exist or that you think may develop. Readers, especially investors, will appreciate the integrity you demonstrate in giving them the full story. Counteract the downside by describing how you plan to avoid, minimize, or turn around the major problems and risks.

The following is a suggested sequence of presentation:

Summary of Major Problems Overcome

Start by summarizing the major problems you have already had to deal with. Give examples of how you attacked and resolved these. Highlight especially innovative and creative approaches you have used to solve problems in your start-up and what was learned from addressing these problems.

Inevitable Risks and Problems

Describe the nature of the problems and risks that your venture will be faced with. Discuss when these problems and risks are expected to present themselves. Discuss how you may avoid or minimize their impact. Describe how you will deal with them. Discuss any threatened or pending litigation or disciplinary action the company or principals may be involved in. Discuss any other legal liability or insurance problems.

Potential Risks and Problems

Describe and discuss, in the same manner as above, the problems and risks that may present themselves. Discuss what circumstances or situations would prompt these to happen and how you would deal with them if they did.

Worst-Case Scenarios

Give a worst-case scenario of all inherent and potential risks that the company may suffer. Summarize the downside and what, if anything, could be salvaged or recovered if these risks did materialize.

Common Mistakes to Avoid

- Failing to identify market barriers

- Failing to identify uncontrollable variables

- Failing to state inability to guard trade secrets (having no patent or noncompete agreements if a key member of your team leaves to join a competitor)

- Failing to give an honest assessment of the downside

- Failing to mention pending litigation or other legal liability problems

Module 14—Financial Data and Projections

Suggested Length   As needed

Objective   To illustrate current financial status and projections. To describe the type of financing desired as well as the amount, payback terms, and potential return on investments.

Note: You should read through this entire module before you start answering the questions.

Pertinent Questions

1. Do you have financial statements for the current year and the past 3–5 years?

   _____

   _____

   Do you have past and/or current financial statements for the company?

   _____

   _____

   Do you have past and/or current financial statements for yourself and other principals?

   _____

   _____

2. If your fiscal year ended more then 3 months ago, do you have recent comparative interim financial statements for your company?

   _____

   _____

3. Do you have copies of company federal income tax returns for the last 3 years?

   _____

   _____

4. What are the financial projections for this venture for the first 3–5 years? (Should be included as an exhibit in your business plan.)

   by month for the first year _____

   by quarter for the second and third year _____

   annually after the third year _____

5. Are these projections based on debt or equity financing?

   _____

   _____

   _____

6. How do these projections compare with industry norms? (Are the costs, revenues, profits, etc., higher or lower than for similar businesses?)

   _____

   _____

   _____

7. What assumptions are the projections based on?

   Give explanations. _____

   Give best-case, worst-case scenarios. _____

   _____

   _____

8. What are the venture's start-up and research and development costs? (Provide itemized list.)

   _____

   _____

   _____

9. What are the costs to produce the product and get it into the market?

   _____

   _____

   _____

10. What are the venture's most significant costs?

_____

_____

How volatile are they?

_____

_____

How do you plan to minimize them?

_____

_____

11. Do you have a cost and cash flow control system in place (your procedures for monitoring and authorizing expenses)?

_____

_____

12. If your venture is a going concern, what are your accounts receivable?

_____

_____

Have you made provisions for writing off bad debts?

_____

_____

13. Have you measured every phase of the venture's operation in terms of profit and loss? (Every department, piece of equipment, and employee should be viewed as a profit center.)

_____

_____

14. What are the margins (difference between the cost to produce your product[s] and expected sales projections)?

_____

_____

Does the projected sales volume justify entering the market?

_____

_____

_____

15. Have you done an analysis of your capitalization decisions?

    lease purchase _____

    tax consequences _____

    cash flow consequences _____

16. Have you done an analysis of your fixed costs versus variable costs?

    _____

    _____

    _____

17. Have you done an analysis of cost alternatives?

    subcontracting possibilities _____

    shared services _____

    in-house vs. out-of-house expenses _____

18. Have you done a break-even analysis?

    _____

    _____

19. Have you forecasted the amount of product you will have to inventory?

    _____

    _____

    _____

20. How much money do you need? How will it be used?

    investment capital (property, equipment, etc.) _____

    working capital (operating, inventory, etc.) _____

    _____

21. What will be the effect on the business of an injection of new funds?

    _____

    _____

    _____

22. Will the money be required all at once or injected over a period of time?

    _____

    _____

    _____

23. Will these funds be raised from debt, equity, or both?

    _____

    _____

    _____

24. What collateral is being offered?

    _____

    _____

    _____

25. Will this be the first request for outside funding?

    _____

    _____

    _____

    If not, who else has invested?

    _____

    _____

    _____

26. Who has been/will be approached for investment?

    results _____

    committed _____

27. How much have you and other principals invested?

    percent ownership?

    _____

    _____

    _____

    What is the rationale for the proposed share distribution?

    _____

    _____

    _____

28. What access to funding sources do you have that you may qualify for? (Check and describe.)

    ☐ state bonds

    ☐ government land grants

    ☐ SBA (Small Business Administration) programs

    ☐ SBIR (Small Business Innovation Research) programs

    ☐ other _____

    _____

    _____

    _____

    _____

29. What are the terms of investment?

    price per share or partnership unit _____

    minimum amount _____

30. What may be the dilution of percentage of ownership of the initial investors?

    _____

    _____

    _____

31. What provisions are made for investor liquidity?

    _____

    _____

    _____

32. What is the payback period?

    _____

    _____

    _____

33. What is the potential return to investors?

    _____

    _____

    _____

How does this compare to what investors are earning from competitors and the industry in general?

_____

_____

_____

34. If there will be any ownership authorized, but not issued:

what percent? _____

intended use _____

_____

_____

_____

35. Do you eventually plan to go public? When?

_____

_____

_____

Do you plan to eventually sell the company to a large corporation? When?

_____

_____

_____

36. Are the end results of financing in line (harmony) with the company's stated objectives?

_____

_____

_____

Does financing allow for better control and flexibility?

_____

_____

_____

Does it provide for needed resources?

_____

_____

_____

37. Have your finances and projections been reviewed by an accountant?

_____

_____

_____

38. What leases, loan agreements, or contracts are currently with the venture?

_____

_____

_____

Subheadings to Include

Funding Request/Terms of Investment
Current Financial Statements
Pro Formas
Assumptions

What to Accomplish

This section is highly scrutinized by potential investors. Most sophisticated investors will undertake an independent financial analysis of the venture. This section must be thorough and convincing. Document the need for funds. Demonstrate that you will use them responsibly and show how they will ensure your success. Use a standard format in the preparation of all statements. Show that your projections are realistic, based on the margins between your cost to operate and expected sales. Back up these projections with reasonable assumptions.

The following is a suggested sequence of presentation.

Funding Request/Terms of Investment

State the amount and type (debt or equity) of funding being sought. Describe the intended use of the funds. Give a breakdown of how the money will be applied, i.e., capital equipment, property, facilities, inventory, and operating costs. Discuss what effect the capital will have on the business in terms of growth and profitability.

State when the money will be needed. Include a graph showing the amount and timing of the funds. Discuss the level of investment already made in the venture. State whether it is funded internally or externally. Discuss the amount of stock or ownership that will be made available but not issued in the current offering. Discuss future funding expectations and the stages at which it will be needed. Describe how the unissued ownership may be used at future stages and how, if at all, this future fund-raising will affect the current offering.

Describe the terms of investment. State the minimum amount to participate. Describe how this offering will dilute the ownership of the initial and subsequent investors. Discuss the rationale for the proposed distribution. Discuss the payback period and potential return on investment. Describe why the investment is attractive and how it compares to other deals within the industry. Discuss any provisions for investor liquidity and the earliest date the investor can recover the initial investment.

State any collateral being offered. Discuss whom you have already approached about investing and the results of the contact. Discuss any access you have to additional investors or funding sources. Discuss what the total exposure of the investor is if the deal goes bad. State what percent, if any, of the investment could be recouped via tax benefits, liquidation, or other means.

Finally, describe how this package fits in with the venture objectives and why the ownership structure being proposed is the most suitable for the business.

Current Financial Statements

If the venture is already in operation, you will need to provide three basic statements:

1. profit and loss sheet
2. cash flow sheet
3. balance sheet

Although it is wise to have complete itemized statements available for the purposes of reviewing a business plan, the reader will be interested largely in the bottom line. For this reason a condensed statement with all three sheets on one page will suffice. A sample can be found in this guide's Appendices. It may also be necessary for you to have past tax returns on hand.

Another helpful tool to include is a budget deviation analysis. This simply shows the difference between your budgeted expenses and expected sales and the actual outcome. Not only is it an excellent internal tool for management, but it also shows potential investors that you gauge expectations against actual developments. Be sure to explain unusual fluctuations. A sample form can be found in this guide's Appendixes.

Describe the terms of any leases, loan agreements, or contracts currently binding the company.

Pro Formas

Your projections should be based on realistic expectations. Be ready to justify all profits or losses for a three- to five-year period. You should provide pro formas for the following:

1. projected income (P&L) statement

2. projected cash flow statement

3. projected balance statement

These statements should reflect the effect of the proposed financing on a monthly basis for the first year, on a quarterly basis for the second and third year, and on an annual basis thereafter. It is also helpful to present these statements in three ways: upside, downside, and probable. Prospective investors also like to see long-range thinking, which implies you plan to be involved and committed to the venture for many years. Probable projections for three to five years are sufficient to carry this section. Include all other statements in your appendix.

It is also to your benefit to provide a break-even analysis and estimated costs and budgets for each department, i.e., marketing, manufacturing, inventory, administrative overhead, etc.

Samples of some of these statements are included in this guide's Appendixes.

When reviewing your projections, the reader will be sizing up the potential to make a healthy return on the required investment. But invariably the reader will be thinking "What is the worst that could happen?" You should be prepared to discuss the alternatives if the downside is realized.

Pro Formas Using Microcomputers

To help you prepare financial projections, we recommend the use of a software package called *Ronstadt's FINANCIALS. FINANCIALS* was designed and developed by entrepreneurs for other entrepreneurs who are neither financial nor computer experts. Since assumptions drive the venture creation process, you need only enter the values for some underlying assumptions about the venture to generate a complete set of financial projections (using an IBM or compatible microcomputer). These include a sales forecast, income statement, balance sheet, and cash flow statement.

The program comes with six industry and two general models— Contract Services, Manufacturing, Retail, Professional Services, Real Estate, Wholesale Distribution, General Purpose, and Standard—and a Personal Finance Model (because your venture's financial status and your personal financial condition are intertwined).

Assumptions

Assumptions are a natural part of predicting the future, especially regarding economics, markets, and financial projections. Your projections are only as good as the assumptions on which the projections are based. The trick is in making reasonable assumptions that those concerned with the start-up feel are valid. Use this section of your business plan to state the assumptions you are making. Discuss why you feel they are valid and what alternatives you may pursue if they do not materialize.

Listed below are some considerations you may have to address when discussing what you are basing your assumptions on:

- Inventory turnover
- Accounts receivable collection period (and bad debt projections)
- Accounts payable payment period
- Purchasing in volume
- Extent of start-up and future capital expenditures
- Useful life of company's assets and related depreciation schedules
- Interest rates on debt
- Effective income tax rate
- Expected capacity and utilization of plant and equipment; availability of suppliers and components
- Variable levels of production based on downtime, holidays, number of shifts and employees, percentage of overtime, etc. (How are you arriving at your maximum output?)
- Sales and share of the market based on characteristics of market, penetration strategies, pricing, competition, and trends of the industry
- Growth and success based on management training and learning curve
  - addition of specialized personnel
  - salaries, commissions, profit-sharing levels
- Sales by markets and products; margins of each

**Common Mistakes
to Avoid**

■ Failing to provide a cash flow analysis and other financial statements

■ Making unrealistic sales and profit projections

■ Failing to make reasonable assumptions (or to show what you are basing your projections on)

■ Underestimating operating expenses, taxes, and other "hidden" costs

■ Leaving the terms of the deal—minimum investment, return on investment, payback period, etc.—unclear

■ Taking too high a risk considering the potential return being offered

■ Planning to spend too much on salaries, office furnishings, and other "fringes" for the start-up

■ Failing to show that the founders (and other key people involved) have made a reasonable financial commitment (put their own money on the line)

■ Offering an amount of stock or other return on investment that is not in line with the proposed investment (giving up too little in proportion to what you are asking investors to contribute)

■ Failing to explain why the ownership structure and terms of the deal are in the best interest of all concerned

■ Proposing a return on investment that is too low compared with what investors are earning from similar ventures

■ Making no provisions for transfer of investment or liquidity if the investors want out (or the company wants them out)

■ Failing to demonstrate the tax benefits of the investment

■ Failing to project the downside if sales don't go as expected

■ Failing to have your financial statements and projections prepared and/or checked by a reputable accountant (you can bet the investor will)

The Finishing Touches

The Big Test

Does your plan accomplish the following?

1. Makes it clear what business you are in

2. Demonstrates that you are solving a problem or filling a customer need in a unique and special way

3. Clearly identifies success determinants
   - sales margin
   - advertising/promotion
   - price
   - cost control/efficiency

4. Identifies major strengths and advantages
   - credit availability
   - equipment/plant
   - management/personnel
   - existing contracts
   - letter of intent
   - limited competition

5. Identifies major weaknesses
   - location
   - competition
   - suppliers
   - unskilled labor
   - undercapitalization
   - poor market identity

6. Shows that the venture has checks and balances among finance, manufacturing/operations, marketing, management, and other areas of expertise

7. Demonstrates that the timing is right
   - economic forces
   - financing/interest rates
   - market forces

8. Outlines your objectives and time frames and how you will get there

9. Outlines the inherent problems and potential risks involved

10. Clearly states what you will do with the money invested

11. Discusses the terms of the deal, potential return on investment over a specified period, and reasonable assumptions on which the projections are based

12. Summarizes how you will update, revise, and refine the plan as situations and events unfold.

The Investor Test

Are you prepared to address five proverbial questions asked of new ventures by prospective investors?

1. If this is such a great idea, how come no one else is doing it?

   This question is designed to put you on the spot. The investor may be skeptical because, if no one else has tried this or a similar venture before, it may be that there is no money to be made in it. Your answer may very well be "There will be competitors emerging after we pave the way and create a sizable market." They want you to justify why it is a viable opportunity.

2. Why are you in this venture?

   This question is designed to find out what motivates you. Some people want independence; others are more motivated by sheer profit. There are always more reasons to shy away from a deal than to risk investing in it. For this reason investors want to know what you think you will get out of it and what makes you think you can do it. Service to humanity is good and well, but investors want to be assured that you have the confidence and burning desire to be successful. They want to know that you are in business to earn a profit.

3. Have you talked to others in the same or a similar business?

   This question is designed to find out how much you know about the industry. Investors want to see that you have done your homework, that you have a good handle on most of the operation's variables—i.e., suppliers, transportation, location, labor, insurance, etc.—and that you learn from others in the business.

4. Have you tried out the product in the market?

   This question is designed to find out if you are market-conscious. Investors want to know that people will buy the product and that you can adapt to their changing needs.

5. Has your plan been critiqued by an accountant, a lawyer, a banker, a management consultant, and/or other professionals?

   This question is designed to find out if this is a one-man show or if you are a team player. Investors want to see that you can access resources and harness expertise. They want to see that all the appropriate disciplines are actively involved, which minimizes their risk.

The Final Test: Do You and Your Plan Have M.O.R.E.?

Motive—Are you and your team motivated? Do you have the drive and ambition to be successful?

Opportunity—Does an identifiable opportunity exist? Is the opportunity big enough and attractive enough to pursue?

Resources—Are the resources needed for success available, and how will you use these resources if they are made available?

Experience—Have you been in this business before? Do you know it inside and out? Have you recruited experienced people to manage and run the important operations?

Packaging Your Business Plan

Your plan should be typewritten, single-spaced. The headings and subheadings should be clearly distinguishable and easy to follow. Use standard elite nonscript type (except to emphasize significant points). Have a person who writes well check the plan for spelling, punctuation, and grammar.

Have your lawyer, accountant, and other professionals review the plan. Have them sign off on the sections they helped prepare (as an example, your accountant may include his name and company at the bottom of the financial section). You should number each plan and have a place for the signature of those to whom you are circulating the plan. This conveys the value of the plan and helps protect its proprietary nature. If appropriate, include a private placement disclaimer as the first sheet. It is also a good idea to include a personalized foreword to each person to whom you circulate the plan, highlighting his or her particular interests.

Finally, you will want your plan to make a good first impression. The cover should have a rich feel and look but not be ostentatious or overly expensive. You don't want to give the impression that you squander money. The name of your company or project should be printed on the cover.

Appendix A: Supporting Documentation

Suggested Length   As needed

Objective   To provide comprehensive documentation that supports the
information and claims made in various sections of the business plan.

Pertinent Questions   1. Do you have any professional photos of the product, facilities, or
equipment?

_____

_____

2. What contracts have you signed? (Check and describe.)

☐ management, employment, nondisclosure/noncompetition

☐ suppliers, leases

☐ customers, investors

☐ professional counsel

☐ other _____

_____

_____

3. Do you hold patent, trade, service mark, or copyright protection
papers?

_____

_____

4. Have you developed a bibliography of all self-performed or
professional research, studies, or surveys conducted in conjunction
with this venture?

_____

_____

5. Have you charted the venture's sales, profits, and break-even
point by product/service and markets?

_____

_____

6. Do you have a chart that names your major competitors, with their share of the market and annual sales over a 3- to 5-year period?

_____

_____

7. Have you done a competitive comparison chart of your venture's strengths and weaknesses?

_____

_____

8. Have you any samples of your advertising materials?

_____

_____

9. Do you have résumés and personal references from customers, suppliers, bankers, former employers, etc., on each of the principals?

_____

_____

10. Do you have personal financial statements for each of the principals?

_____

_____

11. Do you have job descriptions for major positions and support personnel?

_____

_____

12. Do you have an organizational chart illustrating the lines of authority and responsibility?

_____

_____

13. Have you outlined your management control systems?

_____

_____

14. Do you have a time line chart depicting significant milestones and their priority for completion?

_____

_____

15. Have you listed your equipment and other capital expenditures, with a description and the cost of each?

_____

_____

16. Have you graphed the amount of money and timing of the funds to be infused?

_____

_____

17. Have you done a budget deviation analysis?

_____

_____

18. Do you have current and projected statements of profit and loss? cash flow? balance sheets?

_____

_____

19. Have you developed a budget for each department or profit center?

_____

_____

Subheadings to Include

The following is a list of exhibits that you might include in your appendix:

A. Company and Product/Service Support Materials

   1. Photos of the product, equipment, facilities

   2. Patents, trademarks, service marks, or copyright documents

   3. Bibliography of research, testing, and studies conducted

B. Legal Support Materials

   1. Partnership agreements or management contracts

   2. Agent/rep agreements or employment contracts

   3. Noncompetition/nondisclosure agreements

   4. Equipment, facilities, leases, and supplier agreements

C. Market Support Materials

1. Magazine, newspaper, trade journal articles

2. Marketing, advertising brochures, drawings, mailings, and materials

3. Market share and sales chart, three to five years

4. Competitive comparison of strengths and weaknesses

5. Customers contacted and status (signed orders)

6. Letters of intent

D. Management Ownership Support Materials

1. Résumés of key people, references, and letters of recommendation

2. Management control systems outline

3. Significant milestones and time frames

E. Administrative and Personnel Support Materials

1. Organizational Chart

2. Staff training outline for each department/function

3. Job descriptions of key positions

4. Bookkeeping, purchasing, inventory, and other control systems

F. Financial/Investment Support Materials

1. Break-even analysis of company by product, markets, and total operations

2. Financial statements of company and owners

3. Equipment and capital expenditures listing

4. Graph of amount of funds and timing for investment

5. Budget deviation analysis on operations, previous year

6. Budgets for each department or profit center

7. Additional profit and loss, cash flow, and balance statements showing upside, downside, or extended projections

What to Accomplish   Demonstrate you have done a significant amount of thinking and work in all areas of the venture. Your exhibits will lend credibility to your plan. More importantly, they allow the reader to visualize your accomplishments and goals. Make sure they are attractive, readable, and understandable.

The sequence and format of presentation should be similar to the one above, under "Subheadings to Include."

Common Mistakes to Avoid

- Using exhibits that are poorly reproduced or difficult to read
- Including exhibits that are too technical or failing to provide explanations of how to read and interpret the information (some graphs and charts require a legend)
- Failing to list the source or state on what the information is based
- Arranging material poorly throughout the business plan (most documentation should be used as exhibits and placed in back as reference)

Sample Organizational Chart

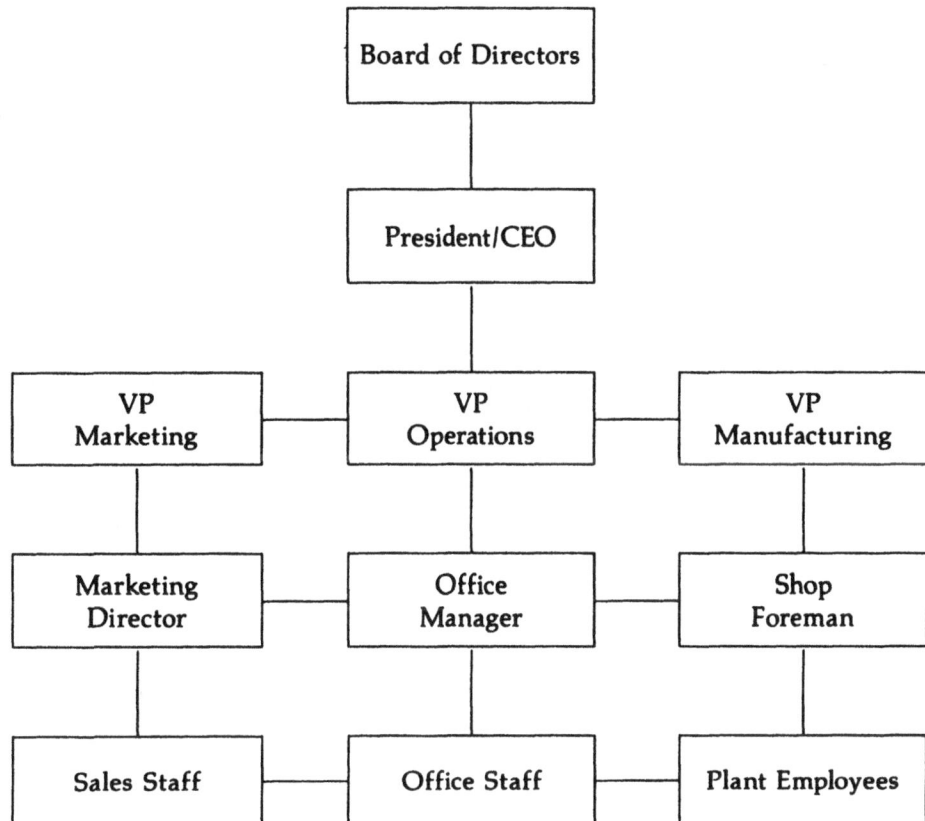

```
                        ┌──────────────────┐
                        │ Board of Directors│
                        └──────────────────┘
                                 │
                        ┌──────────────────┐
                        │  President/CEO    │
                        └──────────────────┘
                                 │
        ┌────────────────────────┼────────────────────────┐
┌───────────────┐      ┌───────────────┐      ┌───────────────┐
│      VP       │      │      VP       │      │      VP       │
│   Marketing   │──────│  Operations   │──────│ Manufacturing │
└───────────────┘      └───────────────┘      └───────────────┘
        │                      │                      │
┌───────────────┐      ┌───────────────┐      ┌───────────────┐
│   Marketing   │      │    Office     │      │     Shop      │
│   Director    │──────│   Manager     │──────│   Foreman     │
└───────────────┘      └───────────────┘      └───────────────┘
        │                      │                      │
┌───────────────┐      ┌───────────────┐      ┌───────────────┐
│  Sales Staff  │──────│  Office Staff │──────│Plant Employees│
└───────────────┘      └───────────────┘      └───────────────┘
```

**Sample Operations
Layout Chart**

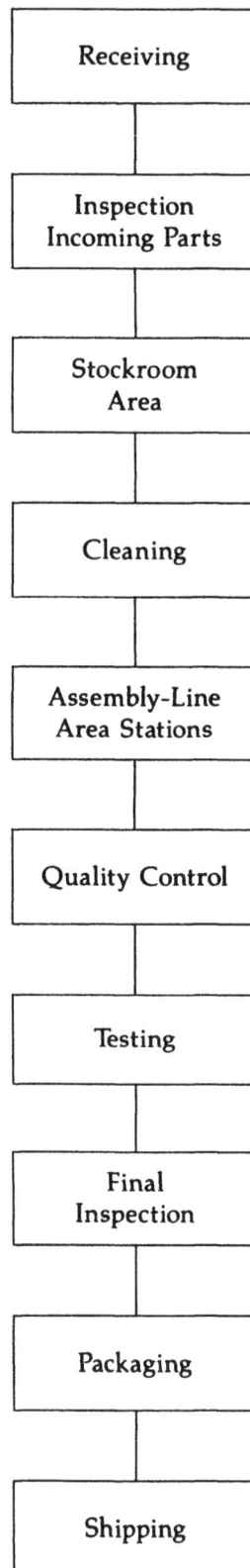

```
                              ┌──────────────────┐
                              │    Receiving     │
                              └──────────────────┘
                                       │
                              ┌──────────────────┐
                              │    Inspection    │
                              │  Incoming Parts  │
                              └──────────────────┘
                                       │
                              ┌──────────────────┐
                              │    Stockroom     │
                              │      Area        │
                              └──────────────────┘
                                       │
                              ┌──────────────────┐
                              │    Cleaning      │
                              └──────────────────┘
                                       │
                              ┌──────────────────┐
                              │  Assembly-Line   │
                              │  Area Stations   │
                              └──────────────────┘
                                       │
                              ┌──────────────────┐
                              │ Quality Control  │
                              └──────────────────┘
                                       │
                              ┌──────────────────┐
                              │     Testing      │
                              └──────────────────┘
                                       │
                              ┌──────────────────┐
                              │      Final       │
                              │   Inspection     │
                              └──────────────────┘
                                       │
                              ┌──────────────────┐
                              │    Packaging     │
                              └──────────────────┘
                                       │
                              ┌──────────────────┐
                              │    Shipping      │
                              └──────────────────┘
```

Sample Time Line Chart

Date	Milestones	Assignment	Alternative Action
1/25/91	Complete mock-up model	Thompson	Drawing
2/28/91	Draft schematics	Thompson	Outline of specs
3/1/91	Prototype working	Thompson/Jones	Subcontract to university
5/1/91	Evaluate/test prototype	Thompson/Jones	Make necessary revisions
	Secure additional seed capital needed	Hendricks	Go ahead or Scrap project
6/1/91	Install customer test site Assemble second unit	Thompson Jones	License to existing manufacturer
6/30/91	Attend industry trade show – distribute literature – demonstrate prototype	Martin	Direct-mail campaign Ad in industry
7/30/91	Complete business plan and marketing plan	Hendricks	Executive Summaries to distribute on limited basis
9/1/91	Determine venture goals	full team	Seek financing Full production Sell project License product

Appendix B: Preparing Financial Projections Manually

To answer the five key financial questions, you must develop three types of financial projections for each alternative venture concept under consideration. The three types of projections (or pro forma analyses) are:

1. profit and loss (P&L) projection

2. balance sheet projection

3. cash flow projection

In addition, you will want to prepare a personal financial statement to better assess your own ability to fund your venture and to show to outside investors/lenders as part of your funding proposal. Any assumptions made in estimating the numbers should be footnoted and summarized on a separate page after each appropriate financial statement.

You can generate a projected profit and loss statement with nothing more than an estimate of future sales and expenses. Certain expenses may increase in proportion to sales increases and should be projected as such. If you have additional information about future production, sales, and overhead charges, you will be better able to project revenues or losses.

The pro forma balance sheet statement lists all of your venture's assets, liabilities, and equities. Enter the appropriate figures as forecasted for the period. This forecast will show you whether your venture has the resources it needs to meet its sales objectives.

Having enough cash on hand to pay all disbursements is essential if your venture is to survive. The pro forma cash flow indicates whether your venture will have sufficient cash for the coming year or whether you will need outside funding. You should fill out the cash flow on a monthly basis so that you can determine the maximum cash required during the period and when that maximum cash need will occur.

WARNING: *If you are preparing these projections with a calculator or spreadsheet, you must understand that the individual statements are not integrated and consequently may contain inaccurate numbers on which you may (unknowingly) be basing important decisions. You will also find it tedious, if not impossible, to produce multiple sets of projections needed to compare different venture alternatives.*

You will be able to make better decisions if you produce these financial projections with the aid of specialized software programs. We highly recommend *Ronstadt's Financials* (see "Related Books and Software" for ordering information).

Projected Profit and Loss Statement

Year Ending _____

Revenue
    Gross Sales $ _____
        Less Returns & Allowances _____
    Net Sales _____

    Cost of Sales _____

    Gross Profit _____

Operating Expenses _____

    Selling
        Salaries & Wages _____
        Payroll Taxes _____
        Commissions _____
        Advertising _____
        Other _____
    Total Selling Expenses $ _____

    General & Administrative
        Salaries & Wages _____
        Payroll Taxes _____
        Employee Benefits _____
        Insurance _____
        Depreciation _____
        Automobile Expense _____
        Dues & Subscriptions _____
        Legal & Accounting _____
        Office Supplies _____
        Telephone _____
        Utilities _____
        Rent _____
        Taxes & Licenses _____
        Other _____
    Total General & Administrative $ _____

Total Operating Expenses $ _____

Operating Profit (Loss) _____

Other Income and Expenses _____

Net Income (Loss) Before Taxes $ _____

    Income Taxes _____

Net Income (Loss) $ _____

Pro Forma Balance Sheet

Period Ending _____

Assets

Current Assets:
    Cash and Equivalents $ _____
    Accounts Receivable, net of allowance for bad debts   _____
    Inventories   _____
    Prepaid Expenses   _____
        Total Current Assets $ _____

Fixed Assets:
    Land   _____
    Buildings   _____
    Equipment   _____
    Furniture   _____
    Vehicles   _____
    Less: Accumulated Depreciation   _____
        Total Fixed Assets, Net $ _____

    Other Assets $ _____

Total Assets $ _____

Liabilities and Shareholders' Equity

Current Liabilities
    Accounts Payable $ _____
    Short-Term Debt   _____
    Current Portion of Long-Term Debt   _____
    Income Taxes Payable   _____
    Accrued Expenses   _____
        Total Current Liabilities $ _____

    Long-Term Debt $ _____

    Shareholders' Equity   _____
    Capital Stock   _____
    Additional Paid-In Capital   _____
    Retained Earnings (Deficit)   _____
        Total Shareholders' Equity $ _____

Total Liabilities and Shareholders' Equity $ _____

Pro Forma Cash Flow

Period Starting _____ **Ending** _____

	Month 1	Month 2
Beginning Cash Balance	$ _____	$ _____
Cash Receipts		
Cash Sales		
Accounts Receivable Collections		
Other		
Total Cash Receipts	$ _____	$ _____
Cash Disbursements		
Inventory Purchases		
Salaries and Wages		
Fixed Assets		
Rent		
Insurance		
Utilities		
Interest		
Advertising		
Taxes		
Other Payments		
Total Cash Disbursed	$ _____	$ _____
Total Operating Cash Surplus (Deficit)	$ _____	$ _____
Additional Funding (Repayments)	$ _____	$ _____
Ending Cash Balance	$ _____	$ _____

Personal Financial Statement

Period Ending _____

Assets

Cash $ _____

Savings Accounts   _____

Stocks, Bonds, Other Securities   _____

Accounts/Notes Receivable   _____

Life Insurance Cash Value   _____

Rebates/Refunds   _____

Autos/Other Vehicles   _____

Real Estate   _____

Vested Pension Plan/Retirement Accounts   _____

Other Assets   _____

Total Assets $ _____

Liabilities

Student Loans   _____

Credit Card Balance Payable   _____

Notes Payable   _____

Automobile Loans   _____

Taxes Payable   _____

Real Estate Loans   _____

Other Liabilities   _____

Total Liabilities $ _____

Net Worth $ _____

Total Liabilities and Net Worth $ _____

Glossary

The following words and phrases are frequently used business terms. Most of them are found throughout this guide. The definitions are our own. The context in which we use them may not necessarily be the same context in which other sources use them.

ADMINISTRATIVE SYSTEMS—internal procedures for handling bookkeeping functions, such as accounts receivable, accounts payable, checking/investment accounts, payroll, and other financial and office functions.

ADVERTISING ALLOWANCES—an arrangement with a supplier, customer, distributor, retailer, or other party to advertise or promote your product in exchange for a reduced rate or higher margins for themselves.

ADVERTISING MEDIA—trade journals, newspapers, magazines, radio, TV, and other forms of communication that reach your customers.

ASSUMPTIONS—preconceived notions or hunches on which you base reasonable financial projections or other probable developments.

BACKUP SYSTEM—procedure and contingency plans for switching to other available equipment should your main equipment break down or become unusable. Switching to other available suppliers should your primary suppliers go out of business or stop serving you.

BENEFICIAL IMPACTS—the positive results your product will have on customers, the community, economy, environment, or other societal force. The problem it solves, the opportunity it fulfills, the needs it meets.

BRAINSTORMING—a management technique used to foster ideas, solve problems, set goals, establish priorities, and make assignments for their accomplishment.

BREAK-EVEN POINT—the point at which all fixed and variable costs associated with manufacturing a product and doing business equal the amount of income from sales.

COMMON STOCK—documents that represent the book value of the business. Also known as *capital stock*, common stock certifies the amount of ownership in the company.

COMPENSATION PACKAGE—the total value a founder, manager, or other employee receives for involvement in the business. May include salary, share of profits, stock or other type of ownership, and other benefits (insurance, auto, retirement plan, etc.).

CONSIGNMENT SALES—having a retailer, wholesaler, or other sales outlet obtain and stock your product at no charge and take a predetermined percent of the gross receipts when the outlet sells it.

CONVERTIBLE DEBENTURES—a loan that allows the debt holder to choose whether or not to convert the remaining outstanding debt into stock at a predetermined price.

COPYRIGHT—legal protection that prevents any party from duplication or using any material or information from a publication without expressed approval from the owners of the publication.

CORPORATE AFFILIATIONS—the position, role, or association a member of your board of directors or management team has with other companies (important to show experience, contacts or possible conflicts of interest).

CYCLE ORDER—as it applies to an inventory control system, a procedure for ordering or replacing a set amount of stock at a predetermined time (every three months).

DEBT WITH WARRANTS—a loan that obligates the company to repay a certain amount of money over a certain period of time at an agreed-on rate, carrying with it the right to purchase stock at a fixed price within a specified period of time. (Differs from convertible debentures in that all debts must be repaid and, in addition, the note holder is given warrants. Under convertible debentures the note holder might not recoup the full loan before buying the stock.)

DEMOGRAPHICS—a profile of the measurable characteristics of a target market, including age, sex, marital status, family size, income, profession, education level, etc.

DIRECT MARKET—the easiest, fastest, and least expensive area or contact with the company's target market for product introduction.

DISTINCTIVE COMPETENCE—the training, skills, talents, education, experience, and performance an individual or company possesses. Whatever it is that you do well that makes you distinct from most others.

DISTRIBUTION NETWORK (or CHANNELS)—the method used to get the product from manufacturing to the consumer. Common distributors are wholesalers, retailers, and manufacturers' representatives.

DOWNTIME—the periods or amount of time that equipment or operations stop running because of service maintenance, repairs, breakage, or lack of business.

EARNING PROJECTIONS—the amount of revenue a business expects to receive from sales, investment, or other income-producing operations within a given period. Usually displayed on an income (profit and loss) statement and/or cash flow statement. See Pro Formas.

ECONOMIC BENEFITS (Trickle-Down Effect)—the positive results your company has on the economy, i.e., creating jobs, injecting new capital into the community, increasing the revenues of existing businesses, etc.

EFFICIENCY RATIOS (Conversion Rates)—as it applies to marketing a product/service, the amount of time, calls, money, ads, mailing, and other marketing activities it takes to make a sale. Example: 50 calls to get 10 presentations, 10 presentations to get one sale.

FIXED ORDER—as it applies to an inventory control system, a procedure for ordering or replacing stock based on predictable levels of activity with production or within the industry (seasonal factors).

FIXED vs. VARIABLE COSTS—fixed costs *do not* vary with the level of output, i.e., salaries and rent. Variable costs vary with the level of output, i.e., supplies and overtime.

GROWTH PATTERNS—the trends and positive speculations within an industry that indicate a promising outlook for business. Growth patterns are based on the overall economic condition, emerging technology, effect of government regulation (or deregulation), and other indicators.

GROWTH POTENTIAL—the increased amount of money, expansion, activity, and other developments that are likely for a company based on the popularity and marketing of its product/service, management skills, industry growth patterns, and other factors.

INDUSTRY PROFILE—the history, participants, total sales volume, trends, growth potential, and other pertinent facts of a particular industry.

INDUSTRY STANDARD—a common basis of operating, pay levels, etc., among companies in the same industry. Example: it is now an industry standard for fast-food restaurants to have drive-up windows.

INVENTORY CONTROL SYSTEM—a procedure for ordering, replacing, and accounting for required stock. See Fixed Order and Cycle Order.

JURISDICTION—the agency or governing body that has the authority to impose and/or enforce regulations.

LEARNING/EXPERIENCE CURVE—expecting performance and results to improve as one gains knowledge and experience. A person's output will be directly proportionate to how much he or she knows about the product, the company, the players, and the industry as a whole.

LETTER OF INTENT—a letter addressed to your company from a customer, supplier, distributor, or other interested party stating a desire to do business with you. (A letter of intent does not necessarily obligate the party writing it but it can be an influential device to sway prospective investors to finance the venture based on evident industry and market support.)

LEVELS OF (MARKET) PENETRATION—how much of the market you expect to reach. Reaching 10% of a nationwide market is a higher level of penetration than reaching 60% of a local market. The percent of the market you hope to capture must be defined specifically. The higher the percent, the more resources it will take to reach and service.

LICENSING AGREEMENT—a contractual relationship with a manufacturer and/or distributor to produce and/or sell your product (usually in exchange for royalties).

MARKET IDENTITY—the ability to create familiarity and loyalty for your product/company in the eyes of the customer through promotions, packaging, labeling, product name, and other factors.

MARKET FORCES (BARRIERS)—ingredients in the market that will affect the success of your product/company, i.e., government regulation, competition, availability of suppliers, etc.

MARKET NICHE—a particular appeal, identity, or place in the market that your product/company has. What you do well, differently from, or better than others in the market.

MARKET SEGMENTS—a separation of markets by broad categories, i.e., by product, by customer, by geography, by industry. Example: marketing computers for the home is a segment different from marketing computers to businesses.

MARKET SHARE—the percent of the target market a company hopes to capture.

MARKET TRENDS—factors that indicate where the market is headed, i.e., changes in customer needs or habits, shifts in population, establishment of new industries in the area, etc.

MBO (MANAGEMENT BY OBJECTIVES)—a management technique for setting goals and objectives and basing incentives on their attainment.

METHODS AND PROCESSES—the technology, operating, assembly, or other features that make the product viable and special.

MILESTONES—significant accomplishments attained in the venture or major junctures the business is steering toward (prototype completion, signing a major customer, etc.)

NONCOMPETE/NONDISCLOSURE AGREEMENTS—legal agreement(s) stipulating that the signer not disclose confidential information about the company and product and/or preventing the signer from joining or starting a similar venture.

OPERATING ADVANTAGES—the strengths of the business, especially as they apply to the competition. May be better equipment, faster production, cheaper transportation, and other factors that enhance the efficiency and marketability of the company.

OPERATING COSTS—all expenses involved in running the business. See Fixed vs. Variable Costs.

OPERATING LAYOUT—how the production facilities will be set up. How equipment will be grouped, workstations located, and storage, tool shop, and other divisions established.

OWNERSHIP INTEREST/DISTRIBUTION—who owns what and how much, i.e., partnership percentage, share of profits, kind of stock, and number of shares.

PATENT/PATENT PENDING—a grant by the federal government to an inventor of the right to exclude others for a limited time from making, using, or selling his or her invention in this country. A patent may protect the concept, process, and/or product itself.

PAYBACK PERIOD—the period of time in which an investor in a start-up can recover initial investment and earn a return on the investment. Most payback periods are between three and five years.

PERSONAL FINANCIAL STATEMENTS—assets and liabilities balance sheet and tax returns for three years (sometimes required by prospective investors of the founders/managers of the start-up).

PREFERRED STOCK—stock granting guaranteed dividends or other rights above that of common stock.

PRIMARY SUPPLIERS—the critical major suppliers of parts, components, and other goods and services to your company, on which your business depends.

PRINCIPALS (KEY PEOPLE)—the founders, managers, board of directors, and other important decision makers of a start-up company.

PRO FORMAS—projected financial performance statements include the balance sheet, income sheet, and cash flow sheet.

PRODUCT APPLICATIONS—the potential uses of your product, perhaps directed at different markets.

PRODUCTION CAPACITY—the total amount of equipment, space, time, or other resources available to achieve maximum output.

PRODUCTIVITY QUOTAS—the amount of salary, commissions, bonuses, or other payments based on specific levels of production and performance.

PROFIT POTENTIAL—the amount of money, less costs of goods sold, that can be made from a product in a particular industry based on predetermined levels of production and set prices.

PROTOTYPE—a model, mock-up, or first assembly of a new product.

PROXIMITY TO CUSTOMER BASE—geographical location of a company's target market in relation to the company. Mode of marketing, delivery, and service is considered.

QUALITY CONTROL SYSTEM—procedures and checks and balances used to ensure the integrity of each product unit.

REGULATORY (APPROVAL) REQUIREMENTS—the restrictions, licenses, laws, and regulations applicable to a product or company, imposed by federal, state, or local government agencies.

RIGHTS AND OPTIONS—as it applies to investment in a start-up, the agreement outlining what, how, and when ownership and payback are exercises.

ROI (RETURN ON INVESTMENT)—the annual percent or money made from investing in a start-up over a specified period of time.

STAGE OF DEVELOPMENT—as it applies to a product, prototype, research and development, short-run production, full production (distribution or other level of activity). As it applies to a company, start-up, expansion/diversification, or other level of operation. As it applies to an industry, introduction, growth, maturity, peak/saturation, decline.

STRAIGHT DEBT—a form of financing a start-up. A loan at a specific interest rate to be repaid over a set number of months.

TARGET MARKET—particular segment(s) of the market at which the product is directed. The initial customers you hope to win over.

TAX BENEFITS—the deductions, protection, savings, and other shelters that result from investing in a start-up.

TRADEMARK—protection of a company's name, logo, or other symbol by the U.S. government, preventing another party from using it.

WORK FLOW/PRODUCTION CONTROL PROCEDURES—the best use of equipment, personnel, supplies, materials, and other resources to maintain efficient operations.

References

Block, Zenas, and MacMillan, Ian C. "Milestones for Successful Venture Planning, Growing Concerns," *Harvard Business Review*, September–October, 1985.

Butler, Robert E., and Rappaport, Donald. *Describing Your Business—An Important Part of Financing*. New York: Price Waterhouse.

A Guide to Preparation of a Business Plan. *The Fundamentals of Structuring and Pricing a Venture Financing*. Minneapolis: Peat Marwick, 1986.

Howell, Robert A. *How to Write a Business Plan*. New York: American Management Association, 1982.

Mancuso, Joseph R. *How to Prepare and Present a Business Plan*. Englewood Cliffs, NJ: Prentice-Hall, Inc., 1983.

———. *How to Write a Winning Business Plan*. Englewood Cliffs, NJ: Prentice-Hall, Inc., 1985.

Manufacturing Business Plan. Manitoba: 1985. Small Business Management Systems.

McLaughlin, Harold J. *Building Your Business Plan*. New York: John Wiley & Sons, 1985.

Osgood, William R., Dr. *Business Plan Format*. South Dakota Business Development Centers, 1987.

Outline for a New Venture Business Plan. New York: Arthur Young, 1984.

Ronstadt, Robert. *Entrepreneurial Finance—Taking Control of Your Financial Decision Making*. Natick, MA: Lord Publishing, Inc., 1988.

———, and Shuman, Jeffrey. *Venture Feasibility Planning Guide*. Natick, MA: Lord Publishing, Inc., 1988.

White, Richard M., Jr. *The Entrepreneur's Manual*. Radnor, PA: Chilton Book Company, 1977.

Related Books and Software

Ronstadt's Financials, software for IBM PCs and compatibles that produces customized and integrated financial projections without a spreadsheet. Software plus eight financial models, user's guide, and the book, *Entrepreneurial Finance*, available directly from Lord Publishing for $119.95

Ronstadt, Robert. *Entrepreneurial Finance—Taking Control of Your Financial Decision Making*. Natick, MA: Lord Publishing, 1988. $32.95

————. *Entrepreneurship: Text, Cases and Notes*. Natick, MA: Lord Publishing, 1984. $39.95

————. *The Art of Case Analysis: A Guide to the Diagnosis of Business Situations*. Natick, MA: Lord Publishing, 1977. $12.95

————, and Jeffrey Shuman. *Venture Feasibility Planning Guide*. Natick, MA: Lord Publishing, 1988. $39.95

Word-processing software for *Writing Business Plans That Get Results* is available directly from Lord Publishing. Includes all questions in the book. Send $14.95 to Lord Publishing, 49 Eliot St., Natick, MA 01760, or call 508-651-9955. Note whether 3.5" or 5.25" floppy.

www.ingramcontent.com/pod-product-compliance
Lightning Source LLC
Chambersburg PA
CBHW061326190326
41458CB00011B/3907